POVERTY IN
THE AFFLUENT
SOCIETY

Readers in Social Problems

DONALD R. CRESSEY, CONSULTING EDITOR

DEAN, UNIVERSITY OF CALIFORNIA,
SANTA BARBARA

POVERTY IN THE AFFLUENT SOCIETY

EDITED BY

HANNA H. MEISSNER

PURDUE UNIVERSITY

J. & J. HARPER EDITIONS
HARPER & ROW, PUBLISHERS
NEW YORK AND EVANSTON

CONTENTS

v

PREFACE

THE READINGS compiled in this book are designed mainly to give to the college student supplementary material on a subject which in general has been very much neglected in professional writings and textbooks. The selection is designed to reflect in some measure the interest of American society in poverty and the attitudes towards the poor in three periods of our history. The first part considers the changing attitudes towards poverty in the nineteenth century. The second part deals with poverty during the depression of the thirties. The articles in the third part are typical of the present climate of the rediscovery of poverty and the war against it. The material is selected from government, professional, and nonprofessional publications for readability and nontechnical presentation in the hope that it will convey to the reader some of the characteristic concerns of the time.

I wish to thank the authors and publishers for their consent to republication of the material. The original footnotes in the readings have been omitted and, in readings 8, 9, and 28, italics have been added for emphasis.

H.H.M.

ATTITUDES TOWARD POVERTY IN THE NINETEENTH AND EARLY TWENTIETH CENTURIES

Until modern times poverty has been accepted as inevitable and as the fate of the masses in most countries. It was looked upon as a God-given condition dividing mankind into rich and poor and assigning a fixed place to every one. Not so, however, in the folklore of the new world, according to which it was up to the individual what place he wanted to occupy. There was work, hard work, but work for all, work on the land, in the vast expanse of an unconquered soil and in the developing communities. A man who was healthy, and wanted to, could make a living in early America, although mostly not an easy one.

The American philosophy stressed that in a society where there is work for all, nobody needs to go hungry. Labor and work are values in their own right; anyone who is willing to exert enough effort can acquire a certain level of material *well-being. The Protestant ethic with its emphasis on salvation through individual diligence, virtue, and honest work fitted well the economic beliefs in the individual's power to achieve economic success through his own exertion, ambition, honesty, frugality, and a virtuous life. If he failed in the economic struggle, it was his own fault; idleness, bad habits, intemperance, vices, and other human weaknesses were responsible for his condition. Poverty was an individual matter, and only the individual could overcome it. The excerpt from William Graham Sumner's writings (page 10) defends the extreme individualistic interpretation of poverty and negates any obligation of society to help the poor.*

Yet there was considerable poverty in early nineteenth-century America. This does not mean the poverty of the early settlers—a life full of deprivation and hardship, but self-relying and self-supporting. What is meant are the poor who were called the paupers, or the pauper or dependent classes, and who were looked upon with disdain often mingled with fear.

As American communities grew, so grew the stream of poor immigrants lured by the tale of fabulous riches in the new country. Many of them had exhausted whatever little savings they had, or their health had been broken by the hardships of the journey, or the death of the breadwinner had left their widows and orphans unprotected. Their unfamiliarity with the language made them prey to exploitation and miserably paid uncertain jobs which left nothing for emergencies. However, their plight and the plight of others was seen in the light of individual causes and dealt with correspondingly, with harshness and lack of charity. The extract of the Yates report (page 4), considered as a progressive document at the time, shows some societal responsibility, but also shows the harsh methods grudgingly used to relieve poverty and to deter people from becoming paupers.

About the middle of the nineteenth century, under the impact of industrialization and urbanization, criticism of the purely individualistic approach to poverty became more and more frequent. Writers such as Herman Melville, ministers like Theodore Parker scoffed at the thought that personal diligence and virtue determined whether a man was poor or rich. Dr. John H. Griscom, a pioneer sanitary reformer, drew attention to the shocking conditions in the slums with his book, "The Sanitary Condition of the Laboring Population of New York" (1845). One-half century later, Jacob Riis, a New York police reporter, tried to arouse a lethargic community to the dangers of the slums and the plight of its inhabitants. Around the turn of the century the recognition that low wages are the basis of poverty found its pioneers chiefly among workers in the settlement movement. The excerpt from "Poverty" by Robert Hunter, who as a settlement worker had first hand experience, describes eloquently conditions of labor, wages, and child labor.

The first attempt to examine closely and in detail the lives and working conditions of the workers in one of the principal industrial communities was made with The Pittsburgh Survey, a pioneer piece of factual and thorough social research, conducted under the leadership of Paul Kellogg, the publisher of Charities and the Commons, later known as The Survey, the leading periodical of social reform. A summary of some of the shocking revelations of this survey is found on page 17. The Pittsburgh Survey and the circle around Paul Kellogg were to a large extent responsible for the subsequent multitude of surveys undertaken by government commissions and private organizations in the years before World War I and for much of the beginning of social and labor legislation.

❪ 1 ❫

Report on Laws for Relief and Settlement of the Poor

J. V. N. YATES
The Secretary of State of New York

. . . The poor of this state consist of two classes—the *permanent* poor or those who are regularly supported, during the whole year, at the public expense; and the *occasional,* or temporary poor, or those who receive occasional relief, during a part of the year, chiefly in the autumn or winter.

Of the first class, according to the official reports and estimates received, there are, in this state, 6,896; and of the last, 15,215; making a grand total of 22,111 paupers. Among the permanent paupers, there are 446 idiots and lunatics; 287 persons who are blind; 928 who are extremely aged and infirm; 797 who are lame, or in such a confirmed state of ill health, as to be totally incapable of labor; 2,604 children, under 14 years of age, and 1,789 paupers of both sexes, all of whom, though not in the vigor of life, may yet be considered capable of earning their subsistence, if proper labor were assigned, and suitable means used to induce them to perform it, . . . Of the whole number of permanent paupers, the returns and estimates will warrant the assertion, that at least 1,585 male persons were reduced to that state by the excessive use of ardent spirits; and of consequence, that their

§ Excerpt from reprint in the *Thirty-fourth Annual Report of the N.Y. State Board of Charities for the Year 1900,* pp. 939–963.

families (consisting of 989 wives and 2,167 children) were reduced to the same penury and want; thus presenting strong evidence of the often asserted fact, that "Intemperance has produced more than two-thirds of all the permanent pauperism in the state": and there is little hazard in adding, that to the same cause may be ascribed more than one half of the occasional pauperism. . . .

There are 8,753 children of both classes under 14 years of age, the greater number of whom are entirely destitute of education, and equally in want of that care and attention, which is so necessary to inculcate correct moral habits. It is feared that this mass of pauperism, will at no distant day form a fruitful nursery for crime, unless prevented by the watchful superintendance of the legislature. . . .

. . . The city of New York . . . maintains . . . nearly one fourth of all the permanent poor. . . .

.   .   .

In most, or all of the towns and villages in the state, where there are no almshouses, the poor are disposed of by the overseers in one of three ways: *First,* The overseers farm them out at stipulated prices to contractors, who are willing to receive and keep them, on condition of getting what labor they can out of the paupers: Or *Secondly,* The poor are sold by auction—the meaning of which is, that he who will support them for the lowest prices, becomes their keeper; and it often happens of course, that the keeper is almost himself a pauper before he purchases, and he adopts this mode, in order not to fall a burthen upon the town: Thus he, and another miserable human being, barely subsist on what would hardly comfortably maintain himself alone—a species of economy much boasted of by some of our town officers and purchases of paupers: Or, *Thirdly,* Relief is afforded to the poor at their own habitations.

The expenses for physicians and nurses, in attending paupers, in towns where there are no poor houses, form a very prominent article in the amount of taxation. Pauperism and disease, except in an almshouse, are generally found associated together, and hence it is, that this item of expense is so much complained of in the towns just alluded to.

After a full examination of the pauper system and its various provisions and results, two questions will probably arise for the consideration of the legislature:

The first is—Ought the whole system to be abolished, and the support of the poor left altogether to the voluntary contribution of the charitable and humane, or,

Secondly. If the system ought not to be abolished, is it susceptible of improvement, and in what mode can it be best effected?

The affirmative of the first proposition, viz.: That there ought to be no compulsory provision for the poor, has many powerful advocates. Men of great literary acquirements, and profound political research, have insisted, that distress and poverty multiply in proportion to the funds created to relieve them, and that the establishment of any poor rates is not only unnecessary, but hurtful. It is not the design of this report, nor would it be proper, and certainly it would not be possible in the compass of an ordinary report, to enter into a discussion of the merits of a question which has agitated and divided the most distinguished writers both in Europe and America, and has called forth volumes of facts and arguments in support of both sides of this difficult and perplexing question. . . .

. . .

. . . Every state in the union, and many governments in Europe, have adopted a code of laws for the relief and maintenance of the poor; even in China, the laws of the empire have made provision for their support. All this is certainly no slight proof that the total want of a proper system would be inconsistent with a humane, liberal, and enlightened policy. Indeed it can hardly be urged, that the idiot and lunatic, the sick, the aged, and the infant (and few others, perhaps, should be made the objects of legal support) ought to be placed in this precarious state for protection and subsistence; and still less will it be pretended, that no provision ought to be made for the education of the children of the poor; and though it is true to a certain extent, that compulsory provision for the relief of pauperism has a tendency to impair that anxiety for a livelihood which is almost instinctive, and thus to relax individual exertion by unnerving the arms of industry: yet the consequence by no means follows, that all provision of that nature should be abandoned, because individual cases of its abuse might, and perhaps necessarily, would exist. . . .

Proceeding then upon the necessity and utility of having a pauper system, the remaining question is, "whether our present laws are susceptible of improvement, and if so, in what manner it can be best effected." Before we can apply a remedy with certainty and success, it is necessary to have a distinct view of the existing evils intended to be removed. That our poor laws are manifestly defective in principle, and mischievous in practice, and that under the imposing and charitable aspect of affording relief exclusively to the poor and infirm, they frequently invite the able-bodied vagrant to partake of the same bounty, are propositions very generally admitted. . . . Without intending to enter into details, it will be sufficient generally to state, *1st.* That our present poor laws (as has already been suggested) lead to litigation of the most expensive and hurtful kind, in appeals and law suits concerning the settlement, maintenance and removal of paupers, exhausting nearly *one-ninth* of the funds intended for their relief, in the payment of fees of justices, overseers, lawyers, and constables, and are at the same time productive of much cruelty in the removal of paupers, frequently at inclement seasons of the year, regardless of the claims of age, sex or condition.

The removal of so many human beings, like felons, for no other fault than poverty, seems inconsistent with the spirit of a system professing to be founded on principles of pure benevolence and humanity. . . .

2d. The poor, when farmed out, or sold, are frequently treated with barbarity and neglect by their keepers. More than one instance has stained our judicial records, in which it appeared that the pauper had suffered such cruelty and torture from his keeper, as to produce untimely dissolution. . . .

3d. The education and morals of the children of paupers (except in almshouses) are almost wholly neglected. They grow up in filth, idleness, ignorance, and disease, and many become early candidates for the prison or the grave. . . .

4th. There is no adequate provision for the employment of the poor throughout the state, and no industrious habit can be effectually inculcated under our present system. This is indeed a very principle defect. Without providing employment for the poor, no system can be productive of much good, either to the public, or the paupers themselves.

Idleness necessarily generates vice, dissipation, disease and crime.

5th. The poor laws tend to encourage the sturdy beggar and profligate vagrant, to become pensioners upon the public funds. The facilities afforded them, in being placed upon the pauper list, operate as so many invitations to become beggars. Overseers not unfrequently grant relief without sufficient examination into the circumstances or ability of the party claiming it, or without the means of ascertaining them.

6th. These laws also hold out encouragement to the successful practice of street beggary.

7th. Idiots and lunatics do not receive sufficient care and attention in towns, where no suitable asylums for their reception are established.

8th. There is an evident want of economy in the disbursement of the public funds, appropriated for the support of the poor in several towns and counties.

.   .   .

The plan submitted, proposes as improvements to the present pauper system:

First.—The establishment of one or more houses of employment, under proper regulations, in each of the counties of this state, with a farm of sufficient extent, to be connected with each institution. The paupers there to be maintained and employed at the expense of the respective counties, in some healthful labor, chiefly agricultural, their children to be carefully instructed, and at suitable ages, to be put out to some useful business or trade.

Secondly.—That each house of employment be connected with a workhouse or penitentiary, for the reception and discipline of sturdy beggars and vagrants. The discipline to consist either of confinement upon a rigid diet, hard labor, employment at the stepping mill, or some treatment equally efficacious in restraining their vicious appetites and pursuits.

Thirdly.—That the excise duties be increased, and a tax be laid upon the owners of distilleries of whiskey, and other ardent spirits, to compose a fund for the relief and maintenance of the poor.

Fourthly.—That *one year's* residence in a county shall constitute a settlement (except in certain specified cases) instead of the present difficult and perplexing requisites of a settlement, which are contained in our poor laws.

Fifthly.—That all orders of removal, and consequently appeals, be abolished; persons who claim relief, shall receive it in the county where they become sick or infirm—the healthy vagrant shall be commanded to return to the county where he belongs; and upon refusal shall be sent to the workhouse, and there treated according to his demerits. It is believed that no order of removal, under the present system, can be so effectual, and certainly none so economical, as the one here suggested.

Sixthly.—That no male person in health, with the use of all his faculties, and being between the ages of 18 and 50 years, shall be placed upon the pauper list, or be maintained at the public expense.

Seventhly.—That severe penalties be inflicted upon all those who bring to, or leave in, a county, paupers, not legally chargeable to it.

Eighthly.—That street beggary be entirely prohibited— beggars of this description, to be instantly sent to the workhouse; and magistrates shall be subject to indictment and punishment, for any neglect of this duty; and grand juries shall be specially charged to inquire into such neglects, and to present the offenders. . . .

. . .

. . . the secretary indulges the hope, that with the aid of the materials furnished, and of such others as may be acquired, some system will be devised, by that honorable body, to relieve the state from the enormous pressure of its pauper burthens, and check the growing evils of pauperism among us. Arduous as the task may be, and it has been declared by able statesmen, to be "one of the most difficult problems of government," it is yet believed to be not entirely hopeless. The improved state of society, the diffusion of useful knowledge, by means of common schools, and other seminaries, the vast tracts of territory yet to be reclaimed and cultivated, the spirit of enterprize and habits of industry which so generally pervade our country, the purity of our laws, the excellence of all our civil institutions, and our remote situation from European conflicts, oppression and slavery, offer strong inducements for believing that pauperism may, with proper care and attention, be almost wholly eradicated from our soil. . . .

⟨ 2 ⟩

What Social Classes Owe
to Each Other

WILLIAM GRAHAM SUMNER

. . . There is no possible definition of "a poor man." A pauper is a person who cannot earn his living; whose pro-

§ William Graham Sumner, *What Social Classes Owe to Each Other*, Harper & Row, New York, 1900, pp. 19–27, 65–66.

ducing powers have fallen positively below his necessary consumption; who cannot, therefore, pay his way. A human society needs the active co-operation and productive energy of every person in it. A man who is present as a consumer, yet who does not contribute either by land, labor, or capital to the work of society, is a burden. On no sound political theory ought such a person to share in the political power of the State. He drops out of the ranks of workers and producers. Society must support him. It accepts the burden, but he must be cancelled from the ranks of the rulers likewise. So much for the pauper. About him no more need be said. But he is not the "poor man." The "poor man" is an elastic term, under which any number of social fallacies may be hidden.

Neither is there any possible definition of "the weak." Some are weak in one way, and some in another; and those who are weak in one sense are strong in another. In general, however, it may be said that those whom humanitarians and philanthropists call the weak are the ones through whom the productive and conservative forces of society are wasted. They constantly neutralize and destroy the finest efforts of the wise and industrious, and are a dead-weight on the society in all its struggles to realize any better things. Whether the people who mean no harm, but are weak in the essential powers necessary to the performance of one's duties in life, or those who are malicious and vicious, do the more mischief, is the question not easy to answer.

Under the names of the poor and the weak, the negligent, shiftless, inefficient, silly, and imprudent are fastened upon the industrious and prudent as a responsibility and a duty. On the one side, the terms are extended to cover the idle, intemperate, and vicious, who, by the combination, gain credit which they do not deserve, and which they could not get if they stood alone. On the other hand, the terms are extended to include wage-receivers of the humblest rank, who are degraded by the combination. . . .

The humanitarians, philanthropists, and reformers, looking at the facts of life as they present themselves, find enough which is sad and unpromising in the condition of many members of society. They see wealth and poverty side by side. They note great inequality of social position and social chances. They eagerly set about the attempt to account for what they see, and to devise schemes for remedying what they do not like. In their eagerness to recommend the less fortunate classes to pity and consideration they forget all about the rights of other classes; they gloss over all the faults of the classes in question, and they exaggerate their misfortunes and their virtues. . . . When I have read certain of these discussions I have thought that it must be quite disreputable to be respectable, quite dishonest to own property, quite unjust to go one's own way and earn one's own living, and that the only really admirable person was the good-for-nothing. The man who by his own effort raises himself above poverty appears, in these discussions, to be of no account. The man who has done nothing to raise himself above poverty finds that the social doctors flock about him, bringing the capital which they have collected from the other class, and promising him the aid of the State to give him what the other had to work for. In all these schemes and projects the organized intervention of society through the State is either planned or hoped for, and the State is thus made to become the protector and guardian of certain classes. . . . On the theories of the social philosophers to whom I have referred we should get a new maxim of judicious living: Poverty is the best policy. If you get wealth, you will have to support other people; if you do not get wealth, it will be the duty of other people to support you.

. . .

That the only social improvements which are now conceivable lie in the direction of more complete realization of a society of free men united by contract, are points which cannot be controverted. It follows . . . that one man, in a free state, cannot claim help from, and cannot be charged to give help to, another.

. . .

. . . If any one thinks that there are or ought to be somewhere in society guarantees that no man shall suffer hardship, let him understand that there can be no such guarantees, unless other men give them—that is, unless we go back to slavery, and make one man's effort conduce to another man's welfare. Of course, if a speculator breaks loose from science and history, and plans out an ideal society in which all the conditions are to be different, he is a lawgiver or prophet, and those may listen to him who have leisure.

(3)

Low Wages and Child Labor

ROBERT HUNTER

. . . While $624 a year is probably not too much for New York City, it is, nevertheless, an estimate which could not apply, with equal fairness, to all of the industrial states of the North. When one gets below these figures, however, every dollar cut off may mean depriving a family of the necessity of life, in times of health even, and unquestionably in times of sickness. . . .

. . .

Testimony was given before the Industrial Commission showing that the 150,000 track hands, working on the railroads of the United States, received wages ranging from 47½ cents a day, in the South, to $1.25 a day in the North. About half of these men are not employed in the winter, so that their yearly wages are further reduced by a period of idleness. But, leaving that out of account, the sum received in the South would amount to less than $150 a year, and the yearly wage in the North would amount to less than $375.

§ Robert Hunter, *Poverty*, Macmillan, New York, 1904, pp. 51-55, 231-238.

The same witness testified that these wages were also paid to the carmen and shopmen in the North and South. There were 200,000 men employed in these latter trades. Before the same Commission testimony was given concerning the wages of the street-car employees. For these workers the wages ranged from $320 a year to $460 . . . According to the United States census for 1900, 11 per cent of the male workers over sixteen years of age, employed in the New England cotton mills, received a rate of pay less than $6 per week, or, about $300 a year. This is the most they could have earned if they had worked every day in the year, which of course they were not able to do. In the Middle states nearly one-third of all the workers are receiving a rate of wages less than $6 per week, and in the Southern states 59 per cent are receiving less than this amount. This will only be received if employment is continuous throughout the year. An inquiry made in Massachusetts showed that the average number of months during which the cotton operatives in Fall River were employed was 9.38. If this proportion would apply to the above operatives, whose wages were investigated by the United States census, their wages should be reduced nearly one-fourth; in other words, their wages would fall to about $225 a year. In the shoe-making industry 51 per cent of the unskilled workers receive less than $300 a year. In the Central states 80.3 per cent, and in the Middle states 87 per cent of these workers receive less than $300. . . .

. . .

The fact that over 2,000,000 male wage earners in the United States were unemployed from four to six months during the year 1900 would alone warrant the estimate that 10,000,000 persons are in poverty. . . .

Not less than eighty thousand children, most of whom are little girls, are at present employed in the textile mills of this country. In the South there are now six times as many children at work as there were twenty years ago. Child labor is increasing yearly in that section of the country. Each year more little ones are brought in from the fields and hills to live in the degrading and demoralizing atmosphere of the mill towns. Each year more great mills are being built to reap the profits which these little hands make possible.

. . .

Many children work all night—"in the maddening racket of the machinery, in an atmosphere insanitary and clouded with humidity and lint." It will be long before I forget the face of a little boy of six years, with his hands stretched forward to rearrange a bit of machinery, his pallid face and spare form showing already the physical effects of labor. This child, six years of age, was working twelve hours a day in a country which has established in many industries an eight-hour day for men. The twelve-hour day is almost universal in the South, and about twenty-five thousand children are now employed on twelve-hour shifts in the mills of the various Southern states. The wages of one of these children, however large, could not compensate the child for the injury this monstrous and unnatural labor does him; but the pay which the child receives is not enough, in many instances, even to feed him properly. If the children fall ill, they are docked for loss of time. And if, "for indisposition of fatigue," they knock a day off, there is a man hired (by the mill) especially for this purpose, who rides from house to house to find out what is the matter with them, to urge them to rise, and, if they are not literally too sick to move, they are hounded out of their beds and back to their looms.

. . .

In the mining districts of Pennsylvania children labor under conditions which are, if possible, even more injurious to them than the child labor of the cotton-mills is to the children of the South. In the mines, mills, and factories, before the furnaces, and in the sweatshops of Pennsylvania, one hundred and twenty thousand little ones were, in the year 1900, sacrificing a part of their right to life, most of their right to liberty, and all of their right to happiness except perhaps of a bestial kind. The Commission appointed to settle the anthracite coal strike of 1902 heard the cases of Theresa McDermott and Rosa Zinka. These children represented, though unknown to them, seventeen thousand little girls under sixteen years of age, who were toiling in the great silk mills and lace factories of the mining districts of Pennsylvania. The chairman could not repress his indignation when these two eleven-year-old children told the Commission how they left their homes to report at the factory at half-past six in the evening and spent at work the long night until half-past six in the morning.

The girls go to the mills, the boys to the breakers. A year or two ago Mr. Francis H. Nichols said regarding these working children: "I saw four hundred lads working in the breakers. One of the children told me, 'We go to work at seven in the morning and stay until six in the evening.'" "Are there many in the breakers younger than you?" he asked one of the children. "Why, sure, I'm one of the oldest; I'm making sixty cents. Most of them is eight and nine years old." Mr. Nichols then asked, "Did you ever go to school?" "To school?" the child echoed; "Say, mister, you must be a green hand. Why, lads in the anthracite doesn't go to school; they works in the breakers!" They do not go to school, but instead they are put to work as soon as they may be trusted not to fall into the machinery and be killed. There is hardly an employment more demoralizing and physically injurious than this work in the breakers. For ten or eleven hours a day these children of ten and eleven years stoop over the chute and pick out the slate and other impurities from the coal as it moves past them. The air is black with coal dust, and the roar of the crushers, screens, and rushing mill-race of coal is deafening. Sometimes one of the children falls into the machinery and is terribly mangled, or slips into the chute and is smothered to death. Many children are killed in this way. Many others, after a time, contract coal-miner's asthma and consumption, which gradually undermine their health. Breathing continually, day after day, the clouds of coal dust, their lungs become black and choked with small particles of anthracite. There are in the United States about twenty-four thousand children employed in and about the mines and quarries. . . .

(4)

The Pittsburgh Survey

. . . The gist of the situation, as we find it, is as follows:

I. An altogether incredible amount of overwork by everybody, reaching its extreme in the twelve-hour shift for seven days in the week in the steel mills and the railway switchyards.

II. Low wages for the great majority of the laborers employed by the mills, not lower than other large cities, but low compared with the prices,—so low as to be inadequate to the maintenance of a normal American standard of living; wages adjusted to the single man in the lodging house, not to the responsible head of a family.

III. Still lower wages for women, who received for example in one of the metal trades, in which the proportion of women is great enough to be menacing, one-half as much as unorganized men in the same shops and one-third as much as the men in the union.

IV. An absentee capitalism, with bad effects strikingly analogous to those of absentee landlordism, of which Pittsburgh furnishes noteworthy examples.

V. A continuous inflow of immigrants with low standards, attracted by a wage which is high by the standards of South Eastern Europe, and which yields a net pecuniary advantage because of abnormally low expenditures for food and shelter, and inadequate provision for the contingencies of sickness, accident and death.

VI. The destruction of family life, not in any imaginary or mystical sense, but by the demands of the day's work, and by the very demonstrable and material method of typhoid fever and industrial accidents; both preventable, but costing in single years in Pittsburgh considerably more than a thousand lives, and irretrievably shattering nearly as many homes.

VII. Archaic social institutions such as the aldermanic court, the ward school district, the family garbage disposal, and the

§ Reprinted from *Charities and the Commons*, XXI (1908–1909) 1035–1036. The address subsequently was published in the *Amer. J. Sociol.*, XIV (1908–1909) 660–667.

unregenerate charitable institution, still surviving after the conditions to which they were adapted have disappeared.

VIII. The contrast,—which does not become blurred by familiarity with detail, but on the contrary becomes more vivid as the outlines are filled in,—the contrast between the prosperity on the one hand of the most prosperous of all the communities of our western civilization, with its vast natural resources, the generous fostering of government, the human energy, the technical development, the gigantic tonnage of the mines and mills, the enormous capital of which the bank balances afford an indication; and, on the other hand, the neglect of life, of health, of physical vigor, even of the industrial efficiency of the individual. Certainly no community before in America or Europe has ever had such a surplus, and never before has a great community applied what it had so meagerly to the rational purposes of human life. Not by gifts of libraries, galleries, technical schools, and parks, but by the cessation of toil one day in seven and sixteen hours in the twenty-four, by the increase of wages, by the sparing of lives, by the prevention of accidents, and by raising the standards of domestic life, should the surplus come back to the people of the community in which it is created.*

As we turn the typewritten pages of these reports, and as we get behind them to the cards of original memoranda on which they are based, and as we get behind them again to the deepest and most clearly defined impressions made in the year and a half on the minds of the members of the investigating staff, it is the first and the last of these results that we see more clearly than any others,—the twelve hour day, and social neglect. Sunday work and night work are but another expression, as it were, of the same principle of long hours of overwork, of which the typical and persistent expression is the twelve-hour shift. Nothing else explains so much in the industrial and social situation in the Pittsburgh District as the twelve-hour day,—which is in fact for half the year, the twelve-hour night. Everything else is keyed up to it. Foremen and superintendents, and ultimately directors and financiers are subject to its law. There are no doubt bankers

---

* These paragraphs are from an address by Edward T. Devine, delivered before the joint meeting of the American Sociological Society and the American Economic Association at Atlantic City. The address is to be published in full in the *American Journal of Sociology* and in the proceedings of the American Economic Association.

and teachers and bricklayers in Pittsburgh who work less, but the general law of the region is desperate, unremitting toil,—extending in some large industries to twelve hours, for six days one week, and eight days the next. There is no seventh day save as it is stolen from sleep. There are of course occupations, as in the blast furnaces, in which there are long waits between the spurts of brief, intense expenditure of energy, but the total effect of the day is as I have described.

For the effect, as well as for the causes of the twelve-hour day, and for a more exact statement of its extent, its limitations, and the exceptions, I must refer to the reports. The unadorned fact remains that in our most highly developed industrial community, where the two greatest individual fortunes in history have been made, and where the foundations of the two most powerful business corporations have been laid, the mass of the workers in the master industry are driven as large numbers of laborers whether slave or free have scarcely before in human history been driven. I do not mean to suggest that the conditions of employment are less desirable than under a system of slavery. What I mean is merely that the inducement to a constantly increased output and a constant acceleration of pace is greater than has heretofore been devised. By a nice adjustment of piece wages and time wages, so that where the "boss" or "pusher" (as he is known in the mills) controls, time wages prevail, and that where the individual worker controls, piece wages prevail; by the resistless operation of organized control at one point, and the effort to recover earnings reduced by skillful cuts of piece wages at another; by the danger of accident, and the lure of pay which seems high by old country standards, the pace is kept, is accelerated, and again maintained. There is one result and there is no other like it.

The adverse conditions are, after all, conditions which naturally, or at least not infrequently, accompany progress. They are incidents of the production of wealth on a vast scale. They are remediable whenever the community thinks it worth while to remedy them. If the hardships and misery which we find in Pittsburgh were due to poverty of resources, to the unproductivity of toil, then the process of overcoming them might indeed be tedious and discouraging. Since they are due to haste in acquiring wealth, to inequity in distribution, to the inadequacy of the mechanism of municipal government, they can be overcome rapidly if the community so desires.

There are many indications that the community is awakening to these adverse conditions and that it is even now ready to deal with some of them. An increasing number of citizens, city officials, officers of corporations, business men, social workers, and others, are entirely ready to enter with others and with one another on the dispassionate search for causes and remedies, recognizing that the adverse conditions are there, recognizing that distinction lies not in ostrich-like refusal to see them, but in statesmanlike willingness to gauge them and to understand them, and so far as it is possible to remove them.

Pittsburgh is unique only in the extent to which tendencies which are observable everywhere have here actually, because of the high industrial development, and the great industrial activity, had the opportunity to give tangible proofs of their real character and their inevitable goal.

SECTION II

POVERTY IN THE
GREAT DEPRESSION

THE *general assumption in the 1920s was that America was as near to the abolition of poverty through the "natural" processes of the market and the ensuing abundance as any society ever had been. The more devastating, therefore, was the experience of the stock market crash of 1929 and the following economic depression, the greatest America had ever known. It brought unemployment to millions who had never experienced unemployment before, and it brought loss of all savings to another large group.*

Private charity which had been the mainstay in relieving temporary distress was totally unable to cope with the situation, and even before Roosevelt took office it had become clear that the individual approach to poverty was not enough and drastic measures were indicated. Great new social inventions of the New Deal were the Civilian Conservation Corps to provide work for youth between the ages of 17 and 23, the National Youth Administration to support needy students with part-time work, the work relief programs for the unemployed, and the Social Security Act.

Substituting work for relief fitted well the prevailing attitudes that relief as such would stifle ambition, striving, and zeal, and would be dangerous to honesty and the integrity of the personality. The excerpt on page 24 from Eli Ginzberg's studies of unemployed men shows how their self-image was distorted while they were long-time unemployed, but changed for the better, when work instead of relief was offered.

The social measures introduced by the New Deal have often been called a social revolution. To a certain degree this is correct, but it must not be forgotten that, for example, the social insurance provisions had been advocated and promoted in the preceding two decades by outstanding social workers such as Jane Addams and social reformers such as Paul Kellogg, I. M. Rubinow, and others. What was new was that a large part of the general public was now underwriting the introduction of social security legislation. Prevention of destitution by giving people a right to economic benefits in cases of unemployment, old age, widowhood—factors looked upon as main contributors to poverty—was considered by many as an all-encompassing remedy. An abundant economy would do the rest.

Excerpts from President Franklin Delano Roosevelt's famous Second Inaugural Address are reprinted on page 31. The Social Security Act was declared constitutional on August 14, 1937, by the Supreme Court; a brief excerpt from this decision is included on page 31. It is interesting to note here that the Supreme Court deviated from a purely legalistic interpretation and made socioeconomic considerations part of the basis for its decision.

The right to medical care in the form of a comprehensive health insurance (the oldest compulsory social insurance form in the European countries) fell by the wayside due to the strong opposition of the medical profession, the drug houses, associations of manufacturers and taxpayers, chambers of commerce, etc. (As we are going to press the "medicare bill" was signed by President Johnson on July 30, 1965. It provides limited medical benefits for insured persons over 65 years of age.) However, the extension of the provisions of the Social Security Act continued under the following administrations regardless of party association.

When the Act was passed in 1935, the insurance part made provision only for the covered wage earner upon retirement and to a limited degree for the unemployed. The adaptation from Eveline Burns' article (page 35) spells out the original provisions. The following groups were added: in 1939, the survivors of the covered wage earner; in 1956, insured disabled wage earners between ages 50 and 64; and in 1960, the 50-year age limit for disability benefits was eliminated.

The public assistance program with its emphasis on need *added a new category in 1950, the Permanently and Totally Handicapped, and in 1961, an extension of the Aid to Dependent Children program to include families with long term unemployed heads. Most recently nearly all the States accepted a medical assistance program for needy persons over 65 years of age. As we will see however, in the next part, the American dream of a society where poverty does not exist has not been reached despite alleged affluence of our present society.*

❨ 5 ❩

The Unemployed

ELI GINZBERG

. . . During the unprecedented expansion of the United States in the late nineteenth and the early twentieth century, a man, if willing to work, had little reason to be unemployed. Hence the public came to look upon the unemployed in much the same light as the hobo, the alcoholic, the criminal.

After the stock market collapse in the fall of 1929, the ranks of the unemployed were swelled, not by thousands but by millions. Even the most hidebound conservative began to realize that there was more to unemployment than the economic or moral failings of an individual. But old attitudes give way slowly. People were willing to admit that the unemployed were the innocent victims of industrial decline, but they suspected that many victims, especially those on Relief, found their new state to their liking. Ordinary folk have to work hard for room and board, while the unemployed got both for the asking. They wouldn't have been normal if they hadn't liked the handout.

The Relief programs of the 1930s were greatly influenced by this widespread conviction that the unemployed were glad to give up the struggle and were quick to accept help. What was the experience of our families between the time that the man lost his job and his first application for Relief?

It is frequently overlooked that even in the depth of a de-

§ Eli Ginzberg et al., *The Unemployed*, Harper & Row, New York, 1943, pp. 43-44, 59–60, 62–63, 71–81, 135, by permission of the author.

pression, most workers are still employed. Surely three out of every four members of the working population were employed on the day that President Roosevelt was inaugurated for the first time. What precipitated the unemployment of the unlucky 25 per cent? Were they really unlucky or were they incompetent, untrustworthy, or otherwise deficient?

Seventy-five per cent lost their jobs because of "lack of work." In 10 per cent of the cases, illness was the precipitating factor. About 7 per cent lost their jobs because of inefficiency, i.e., drinking. The remainder were the victims of political machinations, racial prejudice, and the like. Since the Department of Welfare, prior to accepting a family for Relief, undertakes a careful investigation of the circumstances influencing a man's loss of employment, the information about job severance is highly reliable.

Many men lost out gradually. Mr. O'Brien, a construction worker earning about $50 weekly, saw his employer go out of business in 1928. He then found work as a porter in a cordial shop at one-third his former wage. He lost this position in 1931. Construction workers like Mr. O'Brien were among the first to know of the depression. Mr. Shubor's unemployment was really brought about by a combination of circumstances— the general decline in business and the specific decline in his own trade. He was a skilled workman employed by one of the largest silk firms in the industry. Although this firm was able to meet the initial competition of rayon, it was finally forced out of business. When Mr. Finkelstein found his earnings as a taxi driver falling off, he gladly accepted the offer of a job in his brother-in-law's furniture factory. Finkelstein showed great aptitude, but after two years the factory closed its doors.

Despite the severity of the depression, many business establishments would have pulled through had it not been for the death or retirement of their owners. Mr. Burke tells this story: "After steady employment in the stock department of a large firm for more than 8 years, unemployment came suddenly. The company failed after the death of the owner. Unemployment was a great shock to the family, but they had not anticipated that he would have much difficulty in finding another job. It was some time before they realized that they were definitely in the ranks of the unemployed. He took any kind of work he could find, and for about a year succeeded in making a living by picking up odd jobs. He went around to laundries, moving concerns, and would help load and unload trucks. For one short period he worked as an elevator operator and for another as a chauffeur. However, as the depression deepened, odd jobs became more and more difficult to find."

The white-collar workers had a particularly bad time of it. Mr. Dixon had been salesman and assistant buyer for 15 years for a large New York department store. He related that "he had some uneasy years before he was laid off because people in the department were being dismissed. The buyer was the first to go, then a girl who had been there for 10 years, and finally a floorwalker who had been with the firm for 45 years. When it was Mr. Dixon's turn, he was given two months' salary and a good reference. But he lost the money that he had paid into the retirement fund because the Insurance Company had failed and his employer was not responsible." Mr. Gilbert, a bank clerk, had an even worse experience: "Long before his dismissal, he saw other men being laid off. They were always older men with long service, and gradually he understood that when one reaches 40 and has been with the company 10 years or more, one is certain to be let out. One day, about ten minutes before quitting time, his turn came. He was called into the office and told the news. The manager explained that his work had been excellent, but he could keep him no longer and was forced to dismiss him." . . .

. . . One would think that after a family had used up all its savings, cashed in all insurance policies, borrowed to the hilt, it would no longer hesitate to apply for Relief. But such was not the case. Mrs. Berman said "that they were pretty desperate, but neither she nor her husband would swallow their pride and go and make application for Relief. When he sprained his ankle, she decided to apply because he could not even look for work with this additional handicap. Both cried as they spoke of this period. They were without food or money, the children were crying from hunger, and they were quarreling with each other about what they should do, but each was too nervous to take action until Mr. Berman was injured. When her application was turned down, Mrs. Berman went home feeling licked and decided that suicide for the entire family was the only answer. They felt as if the end of the world had come and they almost lost their desire to live."

. . .

During the early 1930s clothing needs were neglected. Fortunately, most clients had reserves, but as their spell of unemployment lengthened, they had need for replacements. Later on, clothing allowances took the form of an allotment in kind or a special cash allowance. However, these did not suffice. . . .

. . .

The tight budget forced most men to withdraw from their unions, lodges, and sometimes even from their churches. Because they did not have a dime for a glass of beer, many men stopped seeing their friends and acquaintances. Not without serious consequences, however, for the isolated man does not hear of job openings.

Short of food and clothing, few people saw fit to complain about the lack of amusements. Most parents had a hard time finding 10 cents which their youngsters needed for the movies. . . .

. . .

In the early days of the depression, Work Relief payments were made from private, city, and state funds. The men who were employed on these jobs did not consider them "Relief." Mr. E. said: "This was definitely not Relief because it was real work and paid $16.50, a sum sufficient for a man to support his family." It was not until the middle 1930s that the Works Progress Administration, operating primarily with federal funds, became responsible for the bulk of the Work Relief program. . . .

Unlike families on Home Relief, whose incomes were de-

termined by need, those on WPA were better or worse off
depending on the work assignment of the man. When men
on WPA earned less than they would have received on Home
Relief, their families were eligible for supplementation from
the Department of Welfare. In 1940, the basic wage of an
unskilled man on WPA was $52.80† monthly; the semi-
skilled received $60.50; the skilled, $82.80. Most men were
worse off in 1940 than previously, because classifications
and wage scales had been revised.

. . .

The great achievement of WPA was to offer work to men
who otherwise would have deteriorated from idleness. But
WPA did more: in many instances it gave them the right
kind of work. "One of the finest things that WPA has done
was to permit men not to forget their skills; this was not
true of Home Relief." Occasionally, WPA improved on the
assignments which men had received in private industry. Mr.
Leibowitz . . . "had always wanted to paint, but had been
forced to eke out a living clerking until his inner conflict
resulted in his having a nervous breakdown. . . . [WPA]
has enabled him to do what he really wants to do. The wages
have not been high, but he is very appreciative of the fact
that he has been able to express himself. He says that many
coworkers have literally blossomed under the kind guidance
of WPA and they are most appreciative."

Artists were exceptions; the WPA force was composed of
run-of-the-mill workmen. Seventy-five per cent of semiskilled
and skilled mechanical and construction trades workers were
given the opportunity to use their skills. More striking is the
fact that work was found for a photographer in his own line;
a lawyer was put to work on briefs; an accountant was given
a set of books to supervise.

Difficult to place were men who had earned their living as
storekeepers, salesmen, grocery clerks, soda fountain at-
tendants. An exact counterpart to their old job was impossible. WPA did the next best thing. It put them in allied occupations: salesmen became clerks; storekeepers were turned

† Approximately $123 in 1964 dollars.

into watchmen. The excess—and it was considerable—had to be assigned to laboring.

A few men, seeking to improve their classification and increase their earnings, attended classes, but this schooling was highly specialized, since instruction was limited primarily to administrative procedures unique to WPA. However, a few men added to their skills by learning from coworkers on the job.

. . .

We learn from contrast. We learn from unemployment the true significance of work. Only when a man is thrown out of employment does he perceive how much of his life is under the dictatorship of the job.

Work establishes the basic routine of modern living. Men must get out of bed, whether they like to or not, to get to work at a stipulated hour. This they must do day after day. Even when they work only a 40-hour week, men see relatively little of their wives and children, for they are away from home at least 10 hours daily. This explains why Mr. Israel "always helped his wife with the dishes, not because he liked housework, but he wanted to have her free in the evenings so they could talk or listen to the radio. While she is preparing supper, he will come out and set the table for her, just to be near her so that they can talk."

What is pleasure to the employed man—to be at home with his family—is a burden to the unemployed. With no job to report to, and no place in particular to go, the man who had previously been at home only evenings and weekends was now constantly underfoot. He could not always be looking for work, for among other things carfare and lunches cost money. Nor could he listen to more than a limited number of refusals per week. Every "no" was a stab.

. . .

Depressed by his failure to provide for his family, the unemployed man suffers additional frustration. He cannot spend his energies in work. He is deprived of the pleasure that a farmer has when he sees the wheat which he has sowed blowing in the wind. And the butcher, the baker, and the candlestick maker also experience satisfaction at the end of a day's work. Even the man on the assembly line or the clerk behind a counter feels that he has contributed something useful. The unemployed man goes to sleep with his strength unspent, or worse still, dissipated in frustration. He has seen the clock go round but he has nothing to show for the hours that have passed.

This is not altogether true, for many unemployed, in a desperate effort to do something, lend a hand at home. They take care of the shopping, the heavy cleaning, the laundering, and even act as nursemaid. If his wife is in poor health, the man can be extremely helpful.

. . .

The work which men do around the house helps their morale and also eases their wives' burden. Some women, able to handle their own work, deliberately encouraged their husbands to help them, because they thought the men would be better off for having something to do. But working around the house was not all profit to the unemployed man. By taking on feminine duties he widened the breach between his old life and the new. His failure was underlined by this transgression of sex boundaries. Some men took so easily to their new work that one must suspect that it fulfilled an inner need. The better adjusted the unemployed man became, the more difficulties he had fighting his way back into private employment.

Many women were distressed by their husbands' failure to provide for the family. They had taken it for granted even prior to marriage that a husband would provide for his wife and children. When a man failed to carry out his obligations, his wife frequently lost her balance.

. . .

To keep a home looking nice with no money available for replacements meant extra hours of labor. Many women did all their laundry and spent their few free minutes repairing and otherwise lengthening the life of their aging possessions.

The women were constantly harassed—they walked long distances to save a penny or two on purchases; they washed and ironed everything; even the heavy sheets; they tried to cheer up their husbands; they helped their children to get along on very little. . . .

The most serious strain was their gnawing fear that they would never escape from their present predicament.

. . .

People's attitudes toward the future were determined largely by their job prospects. Many were willing to make their peace with remaining on WPA for the rest of their lives. After a man has been rebuffed time and again when seeking private employment, he finds some comfort in protecting himself from further hurt. Older men had no reason to keep looking for private employment indefinitely. It was the better part of wisdom for them to realize that they were through. In fact, only 60 per cent of the entire group had strong drives for private employment. Thirty per cent still tried to find jobs in private industry, but their search for employment was not wholehearted. And 10 per cent had definitely ceased looking. . . .

⟦ 6 ⟧

Second Inaugural Address

(January 20, 1937)

FRANKLIN DELANO ROOSEVELT

. . . I see a great nation, upon a great continent, blessed with a great wealth of natural resources. Its hundred and thirty million people are at peace among themselves; they are making their country a good neighbor among the nations. I see a United States which can demonstrate that, under democratic methods of government, national wealth can be translated into a spreading volume of human comforts hitherto unknown, and the lowest standard of living can be raised far above the level of mere subsistence.

But here is the challenge to our democracy: In this nation I see tens of millions of its citizens—a substantial part of its whole population—who at this very moment are denied the greater part of what the very lowest standards of today call the necessities of life.

I see millions of families trying to live on incomes so meager that the pall of family disaster hangs over them day by day.

I see millions whose daily lives in city and on farm continue under conditions labeled indecent by a so-called polite society half a century ago.

I see millions denied education, recreation, and the opportunity to better their lot and the lot of their children.

I see millions lacking the means to buy the products of farm and factory and by their poverty denying work and productiveness to many other millions.

I see one-third of a nation ill-housed, ill-clad, ill-nourished.

It is not in despair that I paint you that picture. I paint it for you in hope—because the Nation, seeing and understanding the injustice in it, proposes to paint it out. We are determined to make every American citizen the subject of his country's interest and concern; and we will never regard any faithful, law-abiding group within our borders as superfluous. The test of our progress is not whether we add more to the abundance of those who have much; it is whether we provide enough for those who have too little. . . .

〔 7 〕

Supreme Court Decision
on Constitutionality of the
Social Security Act

. . . The purge of nation-wide calamity that began in 1929 has taught us many lessons. Not the least is the solidarity of interests that may once have seemed to be divided. Unemployment spreads from State to State, the hinterland now settled that in pioneer days gave an avenue of escape. . . . Spreading from State to State, unemployment is an ill not particular but general, which may be checked, if Congress so determines, by the resources of the Nation. If this can have been doubtful until now, our ruling today in the case of the Steward Machine Co., *supra,* has set the doubt at rest. But the ill is all one, or at least not greatly different, whether men are thrown out of work because there is no longer work to do or because the disabilities of age make them incapable of doing it. Rescue becomes necessary irrespective of the cause. The hope behind this statute is to save men and women from the rigors of the poor house as well as from the haunting fear that such a lot awaits them when journey's end is near.

Congress did not improvise a judgment when it found that the award of old age benefits would be conducive to the general welfare. . . . A great mass of evidence was brought together supporting the policy which finds expression in the act. Among the relevant facts are these: The number of persons in the United States 65 years of age or over is increasing

§ *Helvering* v. *Davis,* 301 U.S. 619 (May 24, 1937). Justice Cardozo delivered the opinion of the Court.

proportionately as well as absolutely. What is even more important the number of such persons unable to take care of themselves is growing at a threatening pace. More and more our population is becoming urban and industrial instead of rural and agricultural. The evidence is impressive that among industrial workers the younger men and women are preferred over the older. In times of retrenchment the older are commonly the first to go, and even if retained, their wages are likely to be lowered. The plight of men and women at so low an age as 40 is hard, almost hopeless, when they are driven to seek for reemployment. Statistics are in the brief. A few illustrations will be chosen from many there collected. In 1930, out of 224 American factories investigated, 71, or almost one third, had fixed maximum hiring age limits; in 4 plants the limit was under 40; in 41 it was under 46. In the other 153 plants there were no fixed limits, but in practice few were hired if they were over 50 years of age. With the loss of savings inevitable in periods of idleness, the fate of workers over 65, when thrown out of work, is little less than desperate. A recent study of the Social Security Board informs us that

one-fifth of the aged in the United States were receiving old-age assistance, emergency relief, institutional care, employment under the works program or some other form of aid from public or private funds; two-fifths to one-half were dependent on friends and relatives, one-eighth had some income from earnings; and possibly one-sixth had some savings or property. Approximately three out of four persons 65 or over were probably dependent wholly or partially on others for support. . . .

. . . Counsel for respondent has recalled to us the virtue of self-reliance and frugality. There is a possibility, he says, that aid from a paternal government may sap those sturdy virtues and breed a race of weaklings. If Massachusetts so believes and shapes her laws in that conviction, must her breed of sons be changed, he asks, because some other philosophy of government finds favor in the halls of Congress? But the answer is not doubtful. One might ask with equal reason whether the system of protective tariffs is to be set aside at will in one state or another whenever local policy prefers the rule of *laissez faire*. The issue is a closed one. It was fought out long ago. When money is spent to promote the general welfare, the concept of welfare or the opposite is shaped by Congress, not the states. . . .

❨ 8 ❩

The Social Security Act

EVELINE M. BURNS

. . . The federal Social Security Act represents the most ambitious and comprehensive attempt ever made by American government to promote the economic security of the individual. The view that the federal government should properly be concerned with such matters was accepted in the United States only with reluctance and considerably later than in many other equally advanced industrial nations. The tremendous unemployment of the post-1929 depression compelled the central government, however, to grapple with many problems previously regarded as the responsibility of local public and private agencies. Among these were the need for relief and emergency employment. At the same time that economic and financial necessity was accustoming our people to federal action in these fields, two groups which had been working for security measures on a state basis were coming to realize that progess would be hastened if federal aid could be enlisted. These were the advocates of old age pensions and unemployment insurance. . . .

§ Eveline M. Burns, "Social Security Act," reprinted from *Social Work Year Book, 1937,* pp. 472–475, by permission of the author and the Russell Sage Foundation.

The immediate step leading to the passage of the Social Security Act was the message of President Roosevelt to Congress on June 8, 1934. Placing among the fundamental tasks of reconstruction the enactment of measures designed to secure individuals against unavoidable economic misfortunes, the President announced his intention of appointing a committee to investigate the problems involved and to develop a program for submission to the forthcoming Congress. The Committee on Economic Security was created by executive order shortly thereafter. . . .

Formulation of a program involved decisions as to the fields of insecurity in which action was to be taken, the type and amount of security to be provided, the distribution of the resulting costs between social classes and generations, the appropriate spheres of federal, state, and local action, and the selection of the best methods—with due regard to probable constitutionality—of putting these decisions into effect. . . .

. . .

On January 15, 1935, the report of the Committee and the draft of a bill embodying the majority of its recommendations were made public. The Economic Security Bill (H.R. 4142 and S. 1130) was introduced two days later . . . in the Senate and . . . in the House. . . . The Act was signed on August 14, 1935.

. . .

As finally passed, the Social Security Act . . . makes possible three types of security provisions: *social insurance benefits, public assistance allowances, and services.* Social insurance benefits, whereby workers become entitled to benefits payable as a *right* in return for taxes paid by them and/or their employers, are provided for in Titles II and VIII (old age benefits) and Titles III and IX (unemployment compensation). . . . Public assistance allowances, based on the "pensions" previously paid in many states to *needy* persons under conditions less invidious than poor relief, are provided for in Titles I (old age assistance), IV (aid to dependent children), and X (aid to the blind). . . . Security in the form of certain types of medical or other services is provided for in Titles V (maternal and child health, services for crippled children, child welfare services, and vocational rehabilitation) and VI (public health work). . . .

In the case of the old age benefits, the Act sets up a federal plan from which certain specified employments are exempted. Title VIII levies excise taxes on employers (payroll taxes) and income taxes on workers. . . . The benefits become payable to qualified individuals who have attained 65 years of age. . . .

. . . All the remaining types of security depend for their realization upon state action. In regard to the public assistance and the service features, the federal government endeavors to stimulate such action by an offer to share in the cost provided that the state laws meet certain standards. . . . While the degree of federal assistance is limited, . . . the states are free to adopt more generous programs at their own expense. . . .

In regard to unemployment compensation, . . . further to encourage state action, Title III makes . . . grants available to aid the states in meeting the cost of administration. To secure these grants the state laws again must meet certain conditions. . . .

. . . The Social Security Act is undoubtedly one of the most significant measures ever passed by Congress. It implies the assumption by the federal government of responsibility for the economic in addition to the political security of Americans as a permanent and not merely an emergency undertaking. . . . The old age benefits plan introduces for the first time on a national scale a system of social insurance benefits which can be claimed as a right and the unemployment compensation provisions will contribute toward a wider adoption of similar benefits for the unemployed.

Being an omnibus measure the Act embodies many different principles and techniques. This has resulted in its being attacked by both opponents and proponents of governmental provison for individual economic security. The former object to it as a dangerous departure from the alleged American philosophy of individual responsibility, as an unnecessarily costly measure, and as an invasion of states' rights by the federal government. The second group criticizes it for failing to provide against many of the major economic risks, for some of the methods of provision, and for the inadequacy of the benefits offered. . . .

It is evident that the increase in security to which the Act will give rise varies from one type of risk to another. The most adequate provision exists in the field of old age insecurity. . . .

Loss of income due to unemployment is less adequately provided against. . . . Even if all states pass laws under the stimulus of the Act, benefits will necessarily be limited to a few weeks. A large residual group remains consisting of those out of work for longer than the benefit period and those who being unemployed at the time of the passage of the Act cannot qualify until they have again obtained work for the required period. To these will be added the unemployed in the occupations excluded from the Act, workers employed by small employers, and those who by working in more than one state fail to satisfy the contributory requirement in any one. . . .

SECTION III

THE REDISCOVERY OF POVERTY IN THE UNITED STATES

W ORLD WAR II *ended the depression, and it was com-monly believed that poverty was virtually eliminated. The general image was one of an affluent society with the highest standards of living in the world which gave everyone its fair share. Admittedly there existed "pockets of poverty," but there were not enough of them to be concerned. Affluence was thought to have had the following effects on the economy. (1) It upgraded the general economy, increased wages and brought prosperity to all. (2) A large welfare program takes care of those who for one reason or the other cannot make it on their own. (3) There has been a decided redistribution of income, with the lower income brackets getting a larger and the upper getting a smaller share. In the 6os, some econo-mists, Gabriel Kolko, Robert J. Lampman, and James N. Morgan, exposed some of those assumptions as false; Michael Harrington, in powerful language, described living conditions of the poor in a popular book.†*

† Gabriel Kolko, *Wealth and Power in America,* Praeger, New York, 1962; Robert J. Lampman, *The Share of Top Wealth Holders in National Wealth,* Princeton University Press, 1962; James N. Morgan et al., *Income and Welfare in the United States,* McGraw-Hill, New York, 1962. Michael Harrington, *The Other America,* Macmillan, New York, 1962.

It is difficult to arrive at a definition and measurement of poverty. While poverty even in modern times is a majority problem on most of this planet, in the United States and in much of the Western World it is a minority problem and, in Harrington's words, a problem of an "invisible" minority. It has always been true that what constitutes poverty in one society is affluence in another. It is especially true today in comparisons between the Western World and the under-developed countries. But it is also true within our own society at different times and in different places. Poverty is relative deprivation—relative in regard to the rest of society. As J. K. Galbraith expresses it in his book The Affluent Society, *"People are poverty stricken when the income, even if ade-quate for survival, falls markedly behind that of the com-munity."*

Seebohm Rowntree in his famous surveys on poverty in England developed, in 1901, a list of necessities, such as food, clothing, fuel, and household sundries supposed to comprise a minimum necessary for survival and stated that people whose income was insufficient to buy those necessities were living in poverty. At that time Rowntree allowed about 73 per-cent of the budget for food if rent was excluded. In determin-ing poverty levels today we follow essentially the same procedure. However, our needs have changed and increased considerably. In a recent study of the Social Security Ad-ministration, the costs of an "economy plan" budget for a family of four are estimated at $3195 annually; food—rent excluded—amounts to about 43 percent of the budget and, if rent is included, to about one-third. Some other recent studies suggest other figures to determine what constitutes poverty. For example, the study of the Conference for Economic Prog-ress † *considers "disposable" income below $4000 annually as the poverty line for families and below $2000 for unat-tached individuals. The Morgan Study calls those families poor whose disposable income covers less than 90 percent of minimum budgets and who have less than $5000 in assets. According to budgets worked out by the Community Council of Greater New York a family of four (2 adults, 2 children of*

---

† *Poverty and Deprivation in the United States,* Conference on Eco-nomic Progress, Washington, 1962.

school age) would need at least $4330. Whatever basis is used the number of families living below *the poverty line is estimated to fall between 17 percent and 23 percent of the American families. The measurements are rough; there are wide varieties in family size, age, health, location, and needs in general. Also nonmoney income, meals, houses, fringe benefits, etc. are not measured.*

The "economy food plan" of the Department of Agriculture allows an average of 22 cents a meal per person for a family of four. This amount certainly does not include luxuries. Furthermore, what are luxuries in the affluent society? an ice-cream cone? a Coca-Cola? a telephone? or even a car? Where is the limit? A woman in those families living on or below the poverty line can rarely take advantage of food bargains which mostly apply to large quantities she cannot buy, or which are not available at the neighborhood grocery. Poor people pay comparatively more for everything and get less value for their money as Caplovitz has shown in his book The Poor Pay More.

Peter Townsend remarks that the theory of poverty has not advanced beyond the early economists. He speculates that one reason for it might be "that the sciences of economics and sociology sometime seem to be imprisoned within narrow specialisms which discount the flesh and blood and the problems of ordinary life. Partly as a consequence, serious misconceptions about the nature and direction of our society are commonly held."† The definition of poverty at which he arrives at the end of this article is even broader than Galbraith's. He concludes "that individuals and families whose resources, over time, fall seriously short of the resources commanded by the average individual or family in the community in which they live, whether this community is a local, national or international one, are in poverty."‡

Reprinted in this section are excerpts from the report to the House Committee on Education and Labor on Poverty in the United States *which give a picture of the nature and extent of poverty, the composition of the poor, and the ethnic*

† Peter Townsend, "The Meaning of Poverty," *British Journal of Sociology*, XIII (1962) 219.
‡ *Ibid.*, p. 225.

and regional aspects of poverty (page 43). Perhaps the most significant findings are the large number of children living in poverty and the vicious circle of poverty: poverty breeds poverty. Excerpts from Lenore A. Epstein's article focus on health and welfare of migratory workers and their children.

The case study of a depressed rural area by Robert Perrucci and Kichiro Iwamoto is a part of a larger research project. It describes factors related to migration, mobility, and retraining which seem to make adaptation to needed changes exceedingly difficult (page 79).

Excerpts from a speech by Edgar May to the National Conference on Social Welfare (1963) describe an experiment he conducted to make the powerful wealthy Americans in some measure understand the other American, the "new" city poor.

⟦ 9 ⟧

Poverty in the United States
in the Sixties

. . . Poverty occurs in many places and is endured by people in many situations; but its occurrence is nonetheless highly concentrated among those with certain characteristics. The scars of discrimination, lack of education, and broken families show up clearly from almost any viewpoint. Here are some landmarks:

One-fifth of our families and nearly one-fifth of our total population are poor.

Of the poor, 22 percent are nonwhite; and nearly one-half of all nonwhites live in poverty.

The heads of over 60 percent of all poor families have only grade school educations.

Even for those denied opportunity by discrimination, education significantly raises the chance of escape from poverty. Of all nonwhite families headed by a person with 8 years or less of schooling, 57 percent are poor. This percentage falls to 30 for high school graduates and to 18 percent for those with some college education.

But education does not remove the effects of discrimination: when nonwhites are compared with whites at the same level of education, nonwhites are poor about twice as often.

One-third of all poor families are headed by a person over 65, and almost one-half of families headed by such a person are poor.

Of the poor, 54 percent live in cities, 16 percent on farms, 30 percent as rural nonfarm residents.

Over 40 percent of all farm families are poor. More than 80 percent of nonwhite farmers live in poverty.

§ *Poverty in the United States: Report to the House Committee on Education and Labor,* U.S. Government Printing Office, Washington, D.C., 1964, pp. 2–5, 7–9, 13–15, 27–29, 31, 66–78, 103–121, 174–177.

Less than half of the poor are in the South; yet a southerner's chance of being poor is roughly twice that of a person living in another part of the country.

One-quarter of poor families are headed by a woman; but nearly one-half of all families headed by a woman are poor.

When a family and its head have several characteristics frequently associated with poverty, the chances of being poor are particularly high: A family headed by a young woman who is nonwhite and has less than an eighth grade education is poor in 94 out of 100 cases. Even if she is white, the chances are 85 out of 100 that she and her children will be poor.

THE NATURE AND EXTENT
OF POVERTY

Measurement of poverty is not simple, either conceptually or in practice. By the poor we mean those who are not now maintaining a decent standard of living—those whose basic needs exceed their means to satisfy them. A family's needs depend on many factors, including the size of the family, the ages of its members, the condition of their health, and their place of residence. The ability to fulfill these needs depends on current income from whatever source, past savings, ownership of a home or other assets, and ability to borrow.

There is no precise way to measure the number of families who do not have the resources to provide minimum satisfaction of their own particular needs. Since needs differ from family to family, an attempt to quantify the problem must begin with some concept of average need for an average or representative family. Even for such a family, society does not have a clear and unvarying concept of an acceptable minimum. By the standards of contemporary American society most of the population of the world is poor; and most Americans were poor a century ago. But for our society today a consensus on an approximate standard can be found. One such standard is suggested by a recent study, described in a publication of the Social Security Administration, which defines a "low-cost" budget for a nonfarm family of four and finds its cost in 1962 to have been $3,955. The cost of what the study defined as an "economy-plan" budget was $3,165. Other studies have used different market baskets, many of them costing more. On balance, they provide support for using as a boundary a family whose annual money income from all sources was $3,000 (before taxes and expressed in 1962 prices). This is a weekly income of less than $60.

These budgets contemplate expenditures of one-third of the total on food, i.e., for a $3,000 annual budget for a 4-person family about $5 per person per week. Of the remaining $2,000, a conservative estimate for housing (rent or mortgage payments, utilities, and heat) would be another $800. This would leave only $1,200—less than $25 a week—for clothing, transportation, school supplies and books, home furnishings and supplies, medical care, personal care, recreation, insurance, and everything else. Obviously it does not exaggerate the problem of poverty to regard $3,000 as the boundary.

A family's ability to meet its needs depends not only on its money income but also on its income in kind, its savings, its property, and its ability to borrow. But the detailed data (of the Bureau of the Census) available for pinpointing the origins of current poverty in the United States refer to money income. Refined analysis would vary the income cutoff by family size, age, location, and other indicators of needs and costs. This has not been possible. However, a variable income cutoff was used in the sample study of poverty in 1959 conducted at the University of Michigan Survey Research Center. This study also estimates the overall incidence of poverty at 20 percent; and its findings concerning the sources of poverty correspond closely with the results based on an analysis of Census data.

A case could be made, of course, for setting the overall income limit either higher or lower than $3,000, thereby changing the statistical measure of the size of the problem. But the analysis of the sources of poverty, and of the programs needed to cope with it, would remain substantially unchanged.

.   .   .

The Changing Extent of Poverty

There were 47 million families in the United States in 1962. Fully 9.3 million, or one-fifth of these families—comprising more than 30 million persons—had total money incomes below $3,000. . . .

Serious poverty also exists among persons living alone or living in nonfamily units such as boardinghouses. In 1962, 45 percent of such "unrelated individuals"—5 million persons—had incomes below $1,500, and 29 percent—or more than 3 million persons—had incomes below $1,000. . . . Thus, by the measures used here, 33 to 35 million Americans were living at or below the boundaries of poverty in 1962—nearly one-fifth of our Nation.

. . . In the decade 1947–56, when incomes were growing relatively rapidly, and unemployment was generally low, the number of poor families (with incomes below $3,000 in terms of 1962 prices) declined from 11.9 million to 9.9 million, or from 32 percent to 23 percent of all families. But in the period from 1957 through 1962, when total growth was slower and unemployment substantially higher, the number of families living in poverty fell less rapidly, to 9.3 million, or 20 percent of all families.

. . .

The progress made since World War II has not involved any major change in the distribution of incomes. The one-fifth of families with the highest incomes received an estimated 43 percent of total income in 1947 and 42 percent in 1962. The one-fifth of families with the lowest incomes received 5 percent of the total in 1947 and 5 percent in 1963. . . .

The Composition of Today's Poor

. . . Using the income measure of poverty described above, we find that 78 percent of poor families are white. Although one-third of the poor families are headed by a person 65 years old and over, two-fifths are headed by persons in the 25- to 54-year range. Although it is true that a great deal of poverty is associated with lack of education, almost 4 million poor families (39 percent) are headed by a person with at least some education beyond grade school. The data show that less than half the poor live in the South. And the urban poor are somewhat more numerous than the rural poor.

. . .

. . . Five additional major categories of families . . . appear more than twice as often among the poor as among the total population: nonwhite families, families headed by women, families headed by individuals not in the civilian labor force, families with no wage earners, and rural farm families.

. . .

The persistence of poverty is reflected in the large number who have been unable to accumulate savings. The Survey Research Center study found that more than one-half of the aged poor in 1959 had less than $500 in liquid savings (bank deposits and readily marketable securities), and they had not had savings above that figure during the previous 5 years. Less than one-fifth of all poor families reported accumulated savings in excess of $500. The mean amount of savings used by poor families in 1959 was $120; and only 23 percent of the poor drew on savings at all.

It is clear that for most families property income and savings do not provide a buffer against poverty. . . .

Transfer Payments and Private Pensions

Poverty would be more prevalent and more serious if many families and individuals did not receive transfer payments. In 1960, these payments (those which are not received in exchange for current services) constituted only 7 percent of total family income, but they comprised 43 percent of the total income of low-income spending units. At the same time, however, *only about half of the present poor receive any transfer payments at all.* And, of course, many persons who receive transfers through social insurance programs are not poor—often as a result of these benefits.

Transfer programs may be either public or private in nature and may or may not have involved past contributions by the recipient. Public transfer programs include social insurance—such as unemployment compensation, workmen's compensation, and old-age, survivors', and disability insurance (OASDI); veterans' benefits; and public assistance programs, such as old-age assistance (OAA) and aid to families with dependent children (AFDC).

Private transfer programs include organized systems such as private pension plans, and supplementary unemployment benefits, organized private charities, and private transfers within and among families.

It is important to distinguish between insurance-type programs and assistance programs, whether public or private. Assistance programs are ordinarily aimed specifically at the poor or the handicapped. Eligibility for their benefits may or may not be based upon current income; but neither eligibility nor the size of benefits typically bears any direct relationship to past income. Eligibility for insurance-type programs, on the other hand, is based on past employment, and benefits on past earnings.

The Federal-State unemployment insurance system covers only about 77 percent of all paid employment and is intended to protect workers with a regular attachment to the labor force against temporary loss of income. Benefits, of course, are related to previous earnings.

While the largest transfer-payment program, OASDI, now covers approximately 90 percent of all paid employment, there are still several million aged persons who retired or whose husbands retired or died before acquiring coverage. Benefits are related to previous earnings, and the average benefit for a retired worker under this program at the end of 1963 was only $77 a month, or $924 a year. The average benefit for a retired worker and his wife, if she is eligible for a wife's benefit, is $1,565 a year.

Public insurance-type transfer programs have made notable contributions to sustaining the incomes of those whose past earnings have been adequate, and to avoiding their slipping into poverty as their earnings are interrupted or terminated. *These programs are of least help to those whose earnings have never been adequate.*

Public assistance programs are also an important support to low-income and handicapped persons. Money payments under OAA average about $62 a month for the country as a whole, with State averages ranging from $37 to about $95 a month. In the AFDC program the national average payment per family (typically of 4 persons) is about $129 a month, including services rendered directly. State averages range from $38 a month to about $197 a month. . . .

Private pensions, providing an annuity, are additional resources for some persons and families. . . . While the combination of OASDI and private pensions serves to protect some from poverty, most persons receiving OASDI receive no private pension supplement. In any case, benefits under private pension plans range widely, and since they are typically related to the individual's previous earnings, they are low when earnings have been low.

Thus, although many families do indeed receive supplements to earnings in the form of pensions, social insurance benefits, and incomes from past saving, those families with a history of low earnings are also likely to have little of such supplementary income. And since most poor families have small amounts of property, they cannot long meet even minimum needs by depleting their assets.

The Vicious Circle

Poverty breeds poverty. A poor individual or family has a high probability of staying poor. Low incomes carry with them high risks of illness; limitations on mobility; limited access to education, information, and training. Poor parents cannot give their children the opportunities for better health and education needed to improve their lot. Lack of motivation, hope, and incentive is a more subtle but no less powerful barrier than lack of financial means. Thus the cruel legacy of poverty is passed from parents to children.

Escape from poverty is not easy for American children raised in families accustomed to living on relief. . . . This is particularly true when discrimination appears as an insurmountable barrier. Education may be seen as a waste of time if even the well-trained are forced to accept menial labor because of their color or nationality.

The Michigan study shows how inadequate education is perpetuated from generation to generation. Of the families identified as poor in that study, 64 percent were headed by a person who had had less than an eighth grade education. Of these, in turn, 67 percent had fathers who had also gone no further than eighth grade in school. Among the children of these poor families who had finished school, 34 percent had not gone beyond the eighth grade; this figure compares with 14 percent for all families. Fewer than one in two children of poor families had graduated from high school, compared to almost two out of three for all families.

Of 2 million high school seniors in October 1959 covered by a census study, 12 percent did not graduate in 1960. Of these dropouts, 54 percent had IQ's above 90, and 6 percent were above 110. Most of them had the intellectual capabilities necessary to graduate. The drop-out rate for nonwhite male students, and likewise for children from households with a nonworking head, was twice the overall rate, and it was twice as high for children of families with incomes below $4,000 as for children of families with incomes above $6,000. Moreover, many of the children of the poor had dropped out before reaching the senior year.

A study of dropouts in New Haven, Conn., showed that 48 percent of children from lower class neighborhoods do not complete high school. The comparable figure for better neighborhoods was 22 percent.

Other studies indicate that unemployment rates are almost twice as high for dropouts as for high school graduates aged 16 to 24. Moreover, average incomes of male high school graduates are 25 percent higher than those of high school dropouts, and nearly 150 percent higher than those of men who completed less than 8 years of schooling.

.   .   .

Ethnic Composition

The incidence of poverty today is 2½ times greater among nonwhite families than among white families. About 45 percent of the nonwhite families received incomes under $3,000 in 1962, as compared with 17 percent of the white families. Data from the Current Population Survey indicate that the economic position of nonwhite families relative to white families has not improved during the postwar period (1947–62). The data further suggest the strong possibility that the relative position of nonwhite families may have worsened during this period.

The 1960 census shows that the incidence of poverty among nonwhite families varies considerably by race. While nearly one-half (49 percent) of the Negro families and more than one-half (54 percent) of the American Indian families had incomes below $3,000, only 11 percent of the Japanese and 16 percent of the Chinese families had low incomes. About 35 percent of families with Spanish surname living in the Southwest and 32 percent of the Puerto Rican families were in the low-income range. . . .

Of the 9.7 million families in the United States with incomes under $3,000 in 1959, 7.6 million, or 79 percent, were white; about 2 million, or 20 percent, were Negro; and the remaining 80,000, or about 1 percent, were families of other races such as American Indians, Japanese, Chinese, and Filipino. The 7.6 million white families with low 1959 incomes included approximately 240,000 Spanish-American and 60,000 Puerto Rican families. . . .

.   .   .

Close to three-fourths of all the nonwhite families with low incomes are found in the South, as compared with only two-fifths of the white families. The area with the next largest concentration of low income families is the north central region, where 29 percent of the white and 13 percent of the nonwhite families are found. Relatively few poor families of either color are found in the Northeast or the West.

A much larger proportion of the white families have an aged head than do nonwhite families. While of the poor white families one-third were headed by a person 65 years and over, only 17 percent of the poor nonwhite families were headed by an elderly person. On the other hand, twice as many non-white families with low incomes were headed by a female under 65 years than were white families.

A low level of educational attainment is an important cause of low income status. Approximately seven-tenths of the nonwhite families and six-tenths of the white families with low incomes were headed by a person with no education beyond grammar school.

Low wages appear to be another important cause of poverty for nonwhite families. About 36 percent of all non-white families with low incomes were headed by a service worker or a laborer, as contrasted with only 12 percent of the white families. On the other hand, proportionately more poor white families were headed by a farmer than were nonwhite families. . . .

A considerably larger proportion of nonwhite families with low incomes have at least one child under 18 years living with them in the household than do white families. . . . Approximately 43 percent of the nonwhite families with low incomes have at least one child under 6 years living with them, as compared with 24 percent of the white families. Not only are there more poor nonwhite families with children, but they also have more children on the average than do low-income white families. While almost one-fourth of the poor nonwhite families had four or more children under 18 years living with them, only 8 percent of the white families with low incomes had that many children living with them. It is interesting to note that *while nonwhite families constitute about one-fifth of all the poor families, nonwhite children make up more than one-third of all the children living in poor families.*

Nonwhite families with low incomes are much larger on the average than white families. Over one-half of the white families with low incomes were two-person families, as compared with one-third of the poor nonwhite families. On the other hand, one-fourth of the nonwhite families had six or more persons in the family, as contrasted with only 9 percent of the poor white families. One-half of all the persons in low-income nonwhite families were children under 18 years old, as compared with about one-third of the persons in low income white families. . . .

CHILDREN OF THE POOR

. . . Our population today includes about 66 million children under age 18, distributed among some 27.5 million families. In 1961 the median income for these families ranged from $5,905 for those with one child to $4,745 among the million or so with six or more children. . . .

Current census data suggest, for example, that low-income status is unduly concentrated among the relatively small number of families with a mother and children but no father in the home. These families are seldom found on farms where they would benefit from home produced food and farm-furnished housing. . . .

. . .

The children in nonwhite families are also overrepresented in the roster of the poor, and as would be expected, children in a family whose head is not employed the year round must get along on far lower incomes than children in other families. . . .

In 1962, if the same relationship held as at the time of the decennial census 2 years earlier, 87 percent of the 66 million children under age 18 were living with both their parents, about 10 percent with only 1 parent, usually the mother, and

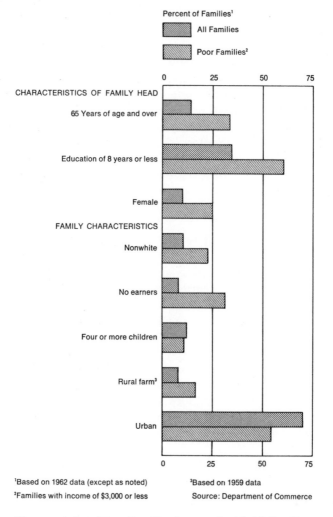

Characteristics of Poor Families Compared with All Families.

the remaining few with other relatives, in institutions, or in foster homes. Nonwhite children were much less likely to have the benefit—both economic and otherwise—of a normal parental home, with 1 in every 3 living with only 1 parent, in contrast to only 1 in 10 of the white children. Nonwhite

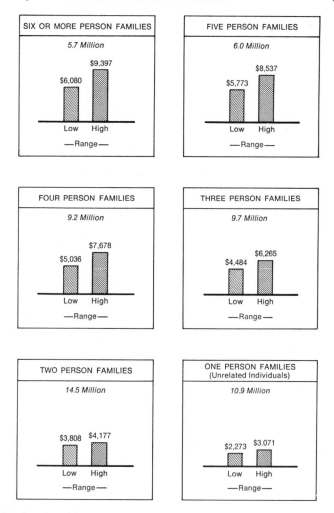

"Modest but Adequate" Budgets. U.S. Department of Labor Budgets for City Workers' Families, 1959.

NOTE: Data on number of families as of 1960. Lower and upper limits of the ranges shown depend on age of head of family, age of children, and other family composition factors.

DATA: Budget data: Department of Labor. Number of families: Bureau of the Census. Conversions to 1960 dollars: CEP.

SOURCE: *Poverty and Deprivation in the United States, op. cit.* p. 18.

women are more than three times as likely to have their marriages disrupted as white women, and more often by separation than by divorce. . . .

INCOME OF FAMILIES
WITH CHILDREN

On the average, in 1962 the mother raising her childen alone had the same number to look after as the mother sharing family responsibility with a husband, although she usually had about 40 percent as much income to do it on. The nonwhite family, though larger, had lower income than the white. . . .

Only 1 in 13 of the husband-white families with children, and even fewer of the broken families (3 percent) had the advantage, in terms of income, of living on a farm. The 2.2 million nonfarm families composed of a mother and her children under age 18 included 5 million "own" children in 1961. Half of these units had less than $2,340 to live on for the year. Four out of every 10 had less than $2,000. What is even more significant is the consistent drop in income as the number of children increased:

Median Income, 1961, of Families with Children

Number of Own Children	Mother-Child Families	Husband-Wife Families
1	$2,550	$6,625
2	2,390	6,615
3	2,345	6,680
4	⎫	6,305
5	⎬ 1,850	5,740
6+	⎭	5,515

. . .

Estimated Incidence of Poverty

A crude criterion of income adequacy—that the low-cost food plan priced by the Department of Agriculture in January

1962 represents no more than one-third of total income—consigns about 71 percent of the mother-child families to low-income status. Even the use of the Department's economy plan, estimated to cost about 20 percent less than the low-cost plan, leaves at 61 percent the proportion of the mother-child families who must devote to food more than $1 out of $3 to get a nutritious diet.

Because larger families tend to have incomes less nearly adequate for their needs than other families, the proportion of children in poverty status is even higher than the proportion of families. It ranges from 25 percent to 35 percent, depending on whether one uses the economy diet or the low-cost food plan as the criterion. As of March 1962, if allowance is made not only for own children but for related children, most of whom are in subfamilies [children who live with both or one parent in families headed by relatives], it is found that 17 to 23 million children are subject to the hazards of insufficient family funds. Even with the minimum estimate of 17 million, there would be 1 poor child under age 18 for nearly every person aged 65 or older.

. . .

By way of suggesting the level of living implied by the present approximation, the income required for a husband, wife, and two children not on a farm would be $3,165 by the more conservative measure, or $3,955 by the more liberal. The mother-and-two-child family, with allowance for the additional relative assumed to be living with the family, would require $2,945 or $3,680.

Some Factors Associated with Low Incomes

The 2¼ million families composed of a mother and her children today represent only one-twelfth of all families with children, yet they make up more than a fourth of all families classified as poor. Together with the 510,000 mothers who are currently living with their children as a subfamily in the home of a relative and who are even poorer, they are raising more than 6 million children. More than a fourth of these families are nonwhite—a reflection of the fact already cited that nonwhite children are more likely than white children to be brought up without a father. Of the families of children with both parents present, only 1 in every 12 is nonwhite.

When the statistics for white and nonwhite families are taken separately, they show, as expected, that the nonwhite families fare worse. Even the white mother raising her children without a father in the home usually does so, however, on a limited income. The median income was $2,675 for the white families and $1,665 for the nonwhite, but the nonwhite mothers had, on the average, nearly three children each and the white mothers slightly more than two.

Nonwhite families in general, despite their smaller incomes, are considerably larger. Three out of every five mother-child families with six or more children are nonwhite, but only one out of five among those with one child. A fourth of the husband-wife families with six or more children are nonwhite, in contrast to 7 percent of those with a single child.

The figures suggest, for both white and nonwhite families, *that it is the poor who have more children—not that the family is poor because it has children.*

Despite recent advances in school enrollment, in 1960 the mothers in broken families generally reported little education. Nonwhite mothers had considerably less; more than one-third had not finished the eighth grade, twice the proportion among the white mothers.

Finally, the nonwhite mother is somewhat less likely to work year round and full time, and when she does she earns much less than the white mother who works all year. . . . Women's earnings generally average less than men's, and those who must adapt their work schedule to the demands of child care find income markedly reduced. Two-fifths of the white mothers who did not work year round in 1961 and one-half of the nonwhite mothers had weekly incomes of less than $30 in 1961. As though to compound this handicap, the mothers without a full-time job were likely to have larger families to care for. . . .

INCOME-SUPPORT PROGRAMS

. . .

With 9 out of 10 workers now covered by the Federal insurance program, the chances are almost that high that, when a father dies today (or becomes disabled), his child will be able to count on some regular income until he reaches age 18. On the other hand, for children bereft of support because the father and mother separate, divorce, or were never married—a much more common family crisis—the possibility of support under a public program is much more limited.

The program of aid to families with dependent children, which is the most applicable to this group, currently makes payments on behalf of children in nearly a million families. Three out of every four of these families have no father in the home. At the end of 1961, payments were going to some 625,000 families with no father in the home—less than half the total estimated to be in need, and possibly not more than 4 in 10. To the extent that eligibility for participation in surplus-food-distribution or food-stamp programs is related to eligibility for public assistance, many of the needy mother-child families who receive no assistance may be barred from these also.

. . .

The overall poverty of the recipient families is suggested by the fact that, according to the standards set up in their own State, half of them are still in financial need even with the assistance payment. The average amount of such unmet need was $40 a month per family and ranged from a deficit of less than $20 in 13 percent of those whose requirements were not fully met to $75 or more in 6 percent.

Inadequacy of Existing Programs

The data outlined for mother-child families as a group suggest how few of the benefits of our existing social programs, as administered, are likely to trickle down to them. In terms of economic progress, we may be well on the way to establishing a "caste of untouchables," with mother-child families as the nucleus. Since most of the mothers in these families are separated, divorced from, or never married to the father of their children—rather than widowed—social insurance benefits to dependents of retired, deceased, or disabled workers are not available to them.

Many of these mothers work in private households, in retail stores, and in laundries and other service establishments not covered by Federal minimum wage laws or unemployment insurance. Three out of every 5 of the nonwhite mothers who are employed are working at service jobs, including domestic work in private households. Two out of 5 of the employed white mothers are clerical, sales, or kindred workers.

A number of these mothers work intermittently, with the result that their future old-age benefits will undoubtedly be minimal. Thus we may already be creating the old-age assistance caseload of the 1980s.

Although more than half the mothers are employed in the course of a year, often they do not hold down a regular full-time job. (Fifty-four percent of the mothers heading broken families were reported at work by the Bureau of the Census in April 1960, but only 1 in 4 of those interviewed in the Census sample for March 1962 had worked full time throughout 1961.)

With day care of young children largely unavailable or in any event beyond their means, the mothers' employment opportunities will be severely limited or children must be left unattended. Manpower and retraining programs up to now have offered little to the woman with as little formal education as most of these mothers have. Rehabilitation programs have seldom provided for child care while the mother is being trained.

Many of the same difficulties characterize the father in husband-wife families with inadequate income. Such fami-

lies as a group can look to even less help from public programs than broken families can. It is perhaps the inability
of the man to earn—particularly among nonwhites—that is
conducive to the marriage disruption or the failure ever to
undertake legal marriage that leaves so many mothers to
bring up children without a father. Research now underway
suggests that families with the father an unskilled laborer, as
well as broken families, contribute much more than their
proportionate share of high school freshmen who rank low
in aptitude.

There are more children deprived by low family income of
their rightful chance at making their way in society who live
with both a mother and father than there are similarly
deprived children living with the mother only. One of the
ways to abate the problem of the low mother-child family is
to take appropriate action while the family is still intact. . . .

A considerable body of data is being accumulated on the
subject of transmission of poverty. Some of the results of
current study are conflicting and difficult to interpret, and
much research is still needed. There seems sufficient basis,
however, for adopting as a working hypothesis that perhaps
the single medium most conducive to the growth of poverty
and dependency is poverty itself. The corollary might be that,
although adequate family income alone is not a sufficient
condition to guarantee that children will escape low-income
status as adults, it is usually a necessary one. There are
people whose only legacy to their children is the same one of
poverty and deprivation that they received from their own
parents.

A recently released study of cases assisted by aid to families with dependent children shows that, for a nationwide
sample of such families whose cases were closed early in
1961, "more than 40 percent of the mothers and/or fathers
were raised in homes where some form of assistance had
been received at some time." Nearly half these cases had
received aid to families with dependent children. This estimated proportion that received some type of aid is more than

four times the almost 10 percent estimated for the total United States population. With education so important these days for any chance at a well-paying job, the educational attainment of children formerly receiving aid to families with dependent children fell well below that of the same age group in the general population. Thirteen percent of the total population aged 18–24 had not gone beyond the 8th grade, but in the sample of families receiving aid the corresponding proportion was twice as high. . . . Similarly, the University of Michigan study reported that among all families with children no longer in school, the children had gone through high school or beyond in 65 percent, but that in only 45 percent of the families defined as poor was this true. . . .

If it be true that the children of the poor today are themselves destined to be the impoverished parents of tomorrow, then some social intervention is needed to break the cycle, to interrupt the circuits of hunger and hopelessness that link generation to generation. . . .

INDIAN POVERTY AND HEALTH

Poverty, as stated by President Johnson in his state of the Union message in January 1964, continues to be a part of the life of the Indian reservation. Some tribes and individual Indians have received spectacular income from gas, oil, and other minerals and from commercial leases, but most Indians are desperately poor.

. . .

Certain aspects of Indian poverty are measurable:

The average reservation family had an income of $1,500 in 1962—one-half the income of $3,000 considered to be a national "poverty line."

Unemployment on the reservations runs between 40 and 50 percent—seven or eight times the national average.

Average schooling of young adults on reservations is only 8 years—two-thirds the national average. A young adult with no more than an eighth-grade education must generally content himself with a low-paying job that requires little or no skill and that leads nowhere in terms of salary and advancement. Much worse is the plight of the Indian, who has less than eighth-grade education, or no education at all. Many Indians lack the vocational training needed to compete for the few skilled jobs that can be found in their home areas. The unskilled agricultural jobs upon which many Indians have depended for years are steadily disappearing as farmers mechanize their operations.

Nine out of ten Indian families live in housing that is far below the minimum standards of comfort, safety, and decency. One or more large families live crowded together in one- or two-room hogans or cabins. Dwellings have no nearby water supply, no sanitary facilities, no safe or adequate means for heat, no electricity, often no flooring except the bare earth.

. . . The 1960 U.S. census counted a population of 552,-000 Indians and Alaska natives. . . .

. . . Three out of five [Indians] are under 20 years of age . . . and the median age is about 17. In the general population, 38 percent are under 20 years and the median age is nearly 30.

. . .

Many adult Indians desire education denied them in their youth. From a beginning attempt in 1955 to develop literacy, 24,000 adults in 140 communities are enrolled in broadened adult education programs.

In recent years special efforts have been made to reduce the high rate of high school dropouts. Since 1946 nearly 70,000 Indian youths have enrolled in special BIA programs to prepare for employment. The employment assistance program principally involves relocation and training. Indians who voluntarily relocate are counseled, provided transportation and subsistence, and helped in finding a job and adjusting the family to the urban environment. Because many relocatees return to the reservations unless they are adequately trained to hold an industrial job, increased emphasis since 1956 has been placed on vocational training for

Indians in the 18- to 35-age bracket. Seven out of ten who go through the full program find full-time employment. Permanent placements during the past 12 years total 17,000, affecting 36,000 family members. In addition, 1,300 older Indians have enrolled in vocational courses under the Area Redevelopment Administration and the Manpower Development and Training Act during the past two and a half years.

Economic Support and Development Programs

During the past 3 years there have been established on or near the reservations some 25 small manufacturing plants employing 750 Indians. BIA programs in irrigation, soil and moisture conservation, forestry, and other efforts to improve grazing and agricultural resources together with road construction and building and utility maintenance provide employment for limited numbers of Indians.

A more immediate attack on the problem of poverty was launched late in 1962 under the accelerated public works program, which has provided employment for 1 out of 20 unemployed. One of the problems related to economic development has been a shortage of credit and a knowledge of its use. Public funds for credit were provided more than half a century ago, but the amount is still small in comparison to the need. The tribes use their own money and carry on lending operations through credit committees. The Bureau of Indian Affairs has a revolving loan fund and backstops the tribal operations with both cash and technical assistance. Tribes have been helped to build and operate sawmills, canneries, and motels and to improve tribal herds. Individuals have been helped to attend school, start small businesses, and improve their homes.

Despite the success of these various efforts, however, there is little employment available on reservations, and the level of education and vocational training of the majority of the people prohibits their competing favorably in a non-Indian work setting.

. . .

Vital Statistics

Forty-two and one-tenth per 1,000 population among Indians and 48.6 among Alaska natives are about twice the birth rates of the total population (22.4 in 1962). . . .

The Indian infant death rate . . . declined 36 percent to 41.8 deaths per 1,000 live births, but is still 70 percent higher than the rate for infants in the population as a whole. The death rate among Indian infants 28 days through 11 months of age was 3.8 times the rate for all races. . . .

Several of the 10 leading notifiable diseases among Indians in 1962 . . . are so minor in their impact on the general population as not to be reported. Among Alaska natives leading diseases in 1962 in order of incidence were: respiratory infections, otitis media, gastroenteritis, pneumonia, streptococcal throat, measles, and tuberculosis.

The Indian and Alaska native tuberculosis death rates . . . have been reduced 46 and 87 percent, respectively, since 1954. The present Indian and Alaska native rates are almost six times greater than the all-races rate. . . .

Nearly one-sixth of all Indian deaths in a year are attributable to tuberculosis, gastroenteric, and other infectious diseases, reflecting, in part, the rigorous environment of the . . . group, the insufficient sanitation facilities, poor and crowded living conditions, inadequate food, and poor nutritional levels.

The percent of the total deaths in a year which are due to these and other infectious diseases is three times higher than in the general population. Nonetheless, the infectious diseases are slowly being displaced by degenerative conditions and noninfectious types. . . .

APPALACHIA

In Appalachia, almost 1 in 3 families lives on an annual income of $3,000 or less. . . . Only 8.7 percent of Appalachian families have incomes over $10,000 a year, compared to

15.6 percent, a figure almost twice as high, in the rest of the United States.

. . .

In 1960 there were 380,000 unemployed workers in Appalachia. These represented 7.1 percent of the Appalachian labor force, compared to 5.0 percent in the rest of the United States. But the deficiency of job opportunity is far greater than these statistics would indicate. For these figures do not take into account the many men and women who, in despair of ever finding jobs, have given up the search and withdrawn from the labor force. In Appalachia, that group is extremely large. . . .

The deficiency of job opportunities in the Appalachian region in recent years is the result of severe declines in employment in mining and agriculture. Between 1950 and 1960 these two sectors combined to release 641,000 workers, or more than half of their 1950 work force. During this period manufacturing, construction, and service employment increased by 567,000 but not sufficiently to prevent a net decrease of 1.5 percent in total employment.

. . .

Education

For every 100 persons over 25 years of age elsewhere in the United States, 8 have failed to finish 5 years of school. In Appalachia, that figure rises to more than 11, 45 percent higher than the balance of the United States. In the Appalachian portion of three States, the figure is above the national average. But in the remainder, the percentage of those who fail to finish 5 years of school ranges from 11 percent to 22 percent.

Thirty-two out of every 100 Appalachians over 25 have finished high school, contrasted to almost 42 persons of similar age in the balance of the United States. Thus, within its 25 and older population, 23 percent fewer high school graduates can be found than in the rest of the United States. No section of Appalachia reaches the national norm for the rest of the United States and one State dips to 58 percent below that norm.

. . .

Another index of poverty in the area is the condition of housing. In Appalachia, 26.6 percent of the homes need major repairs and 7.5 percent are in such a dilapidated condition that they endanger the health and safety of the families. The comparable percentages for the rest of the United States are 18.1 and 4.7, respectively. The situation is more aggravated in rural areas. Here, almost 1 out of 4 homes has basic deficiencies that require correction to provide adequate housing; 1 out of 10 is dilapidated. More than half of the farm homes lack adequate plumbing. In the rural sections of one State almost half of the homes need either major repairs or replacement, and more than three-fourths of the farm homes lack complete plumbing.

. . .

The most complete set of figures available on Appalachian distress is the tally of federally supported programs of public assistance. . . . Here in Appalachia, the percentage of total population receiving Federal assistance is 45 percent above the figure for the rest of the Nation. . . .

Particular programs show a considerable range of difference from the rest of the Nation in the percent of total population receiving aid—but in every case, Appalachia is higher. . . . This is also true of more than 1 million in the region who receive assistance in the form of surplus food. Appalachia's 8.5 percent of the U.S. population receive 17 percent of this form of aid.

The total monthly Federal expenditure in Appalachia for welfare—including food programs, but excluding all programs to which the recipients have contributed, such as unemployment compensation and social security—is conservatively set at $41 million. In 1 year the figure mounts to almost $500 million; in 10 years to almost $5 billion. . . .†

† President Johnson signed the Aid to Appalachia Bill on March 8, 1965. The bill allots $1.1 billion to combat poverty in 11 Appalachian states. The money is provided for highway construction, new hospitals, restoration of strip-mine areas, vocational education and soil restoration.

❰ 10 ❱

Health and Welfare Problems

LENORE A. EPSTEIN

. . . Of the 33 million poor in the Nation, some 3 million children and about 4 million adults are receiving public assistance. In addition, about 3.0–3.5 million persons are in financial need and receive surplus foods but no cash assistance from a public agency.

Medical care cost problems weigh heavily on many of them, particularly the aged. Even more serious for the future is the large number of mothers who are indigent or medically indigent—currently estimated at 35 percent of pregnant mothers in cities with a population of 100,000 or more. An increasing number of these mothers receive little or no prenatal care and inadequate postnatal care. Despite the fact that the rate for maternal deaths had dropped to 3.7 per 10,000 live births for the United States as a whole, the rate for nonwhite women was about four times that for white women. This difference points to an area needing substantial improvement.

In a national survey of aid to families with dependent children made at the end of 1961, 11 out of every 100 children receiving aid were recorded as having a physical or mental defect according to professional opinion, and at least that many were listed, on the basis of nonprofessional opinion, as having one or more defects. Children in low-income families not receiving assistance may well have as many defects.

§ Lenore A. Epstein, "Unmet Need in a Land of Abundance" *Social Security Bulletin,* Washington, D.C., May 1963, pp. 8–11.

Families and children receiving assistance, and other families as well, often need a special service of one kind or another. Although services cannot substitute for income, certain types of service might counteract some of the effects of poverty and thus help to break the cycle of cultural deprivation that is often associated with poverty. In all programs —public assistance, child welfare, and juvenile delinquency —staffing falls far short of need, not only in terms of training but even in numbers. In 1960 the average caseload for public assistance workers was from 50 percent to 100 percent larger than is considered desirable.

About 15 million children have mothers who are working outside the home. Four million of these children are under age 6, and 5 million are aged 6–11. According to a 1958 survey, almost 400,000 children under age 12 were expected to take care of themselves while their mothers worked full time. Although these are the children most obviously needing day-care services, there are others. Children whose mothers are ill, who live in overcrowded slum conditions with no play space, who are emotionally handicapped or mentally retarded, or whose family has special problems—for all these children, day-care services are a needed community facility for their protection.

Existing day-care facilities are grossly inadequate; only about 185,000 children can be served by licensed facilities. There are 11 States—most of them high-income, industrial States—where among the urban population fewer than a fifth of women with preschool children are in the labor force. Yet in the District of Columbia, Georgia, Mississippi, North Carolina, and South Carolina, more than a third of the women with children under age 6 are in the labor force.

MENTAL RETARDATION

The conditions that lead to high maternal death rates are likely also to lead to mental retardation. The dimensions of the problem of mental retardation are clear when it is realized how large a proportion of the population suffers from this handicap. It is estimated that for 3 percent of the population (5.4 million persons) the ability to learn and to adapt to the demands of society is significantly impaired. Constant care or supervision is required for some 400,000. An estimated 15–20 million people are in families with a mentally retarded member. It is further estimated that 126,000 infants born each year will be identified at some time as mentally retarded. By 1970, at the present rate, there will be 1 million more retarded persons than there are at present.

Among those 5 million persons who are considered as mildly retarded, there is a significantly higher prevalence in those population groups whose incomes are low, whose education is limited, and for whom prenatal and postnatal care is frequently inadequate.

About 1¼ million of the retarded are of school age, when mild retardation is most likely to be identified. They represent 11 percent of the schoolage population, but only one-fifth of them are enrolled in special education programs in public schools.

Major deterrents to increased enrollment are the lack of qualified teachers and limited financial resources. (The average cost of educating the retarded is about twice that of educating the nonhandicapped.)

Premature infants are apt to suffer from a significantly higher incidence of death and damage, including mental retardation, than full-term infants. Prematurity rates vary directly with the percentage of women receiving little or no prenatal care. The incidence of toxemias of pregnancy among women in higher-income groups is only 3 percent, but in the lower-income group it is 15 percent. A survey in the District of Columbia showed a prematurity rate of 22.7 percent when the mothers received no prenatal care and 10.4 percent among those receiving prenatal care. A 1952 study in Chicago showed that 65 percent of those in special classes for the retarded came from 11 slumridden areas, out of 75 areas in the metropolitan community. . . .

MIGRATORY FARM WORKERS

Migratory workers are among those having serious problems of income, of health, and of education. The domestic
migrant work force, according to the Department of Agriculture, numbers almost 500,000. In addition, about 450,000
foreign agricultural workers enter the country each year,
mostly from Mexico. There are three major migrant streams
for domestic migrants. The largest, followed by about 250,-
000 workers, is the mid-continent movement made up largely
of Texas-Mexicans, whose home base is in South Texas.
About 100,000 workers follow the Western States migrant
stream, which moves from Southern California northward
through the Pacific Coast States. The East Coast migrant
stream attracts almost 100,000 workers—Southeastern Negroes, Puerto Ricans, and some Texans. This stream moves
north from Florida to North Carolina to New York State and
then back to Florida.

In 1960 about 317,000 domestic migrants worked on a
farm, for wages, for 25 days or more. During the year they
worked, on the average, 157 days and had earnings of $1,016.
Almost two-thirds of all migrants earned less than $1,000
from farm and nonfarm work combined. About 40 out of
every 100 experienced some involuntary unemployment;
about 1 out of 10 were out of work for at least half the year.

One reason the problem of the migrant worker families is
so serious is the number of children in these families—
350,000–450,000. About 225,000 travel with their parents,
and about a third of this group work. More than half the
migrant children lag behind other children in their school
work by 1–4 years. Usually they do not get past the fourth
grade. Seven States have established summer schools for the
migrant children—generally for periods of 4–6 weeks—and
eight States have enacted legislation relating to the education
of migrant children.

Among the migrants aged 20 or over, about 2 out of every
3 have not completed the eighth grade. Almost 3 out of 10

would be classified as functionally illiterate, with less than 5 years of school, and only 14 percent had completed high school. The low educational status of the migratory farm laborers has persisted since 1940, and the low educational level is especially marked for workers aged 45 and over and for the nonwhite migrants.

❲ 11 ❳

The Disjointed Trio: Poverty, Politics, and Power

EDGAR MAY

. . . We have a new poor in this country today, but we are using the old images. Most Americans take their portrait of poverty—that is, if they think about it at all—out of the depression museum. Not only is this dreary canvas musty, but in the light of the 1960s, it is distorted and frequently false.

In the depression, writers, storekeepers, foremen, and even college professors could be found, if not in the soup lines, certainly on the rosters of WPA projects. This economic upheaval produced an impoverished middle class and, specifically, a poor man who lacked one major commodity—namely, money—and the opportunity to earn it.

In my conversations with Americans in different parts of this nation and from different walks of life, I find that many still believe in this hangover-from-the-depression definition.

§ Edgar May, "The Disjointed Trio: Poverty, Politics, and Power," reprinted from *National Conference on Social Welfare: Social Welfare Forum, 1963*, pp. 47–61, by permission of the Columbia University Press.

They believe, or want to believe, that a poor man is a middle-class American without money. Therefore, a temporary cash tide-me-over or a job—for which he may not be qualified—certainly should do the trick. Providing a relief check today has yet to conjure up the educational background, the training, the manners, the habits—in short, the culture traits—of the impoverished storekeeper or jobless foreman of yesterday.

. . .

Now, when I say we have a "new" poor today, the term certainly is not all-inclusive. The aged whose savings are depleted by never-ending medical bills probably are the last vestiges of the impoverished middle class.

Those whom social workers call "multiproblem" families, and whom others refer to in less delicate fashion, certainly were present in the depression. They could not surmount the host of problems they had then and they appear not to conquer them now. But, beyond these two groups, we have two distinct additions in the poverty category; frequently they overlap.

The first of these is the latest American immigrant to our urban centers. Ironically, he is a native American who finds himself a displaced person. He has a history of poverty that has been given a newness because it has been transplanted from the scattered shacks and tenant farms of rural America to the tenement ghettos of the city. I am talking, of course, about the American Negro whose trek from the rural South is not so much in order to find equality as, realistically, it is to obtain less inequality than he found in the place from which he came. The narrower the difference between these places, the greater has been his acceleration toward relief.

He comes at a time when the urban economy has no room for the scanty equipment he offers it. He is a nineteenth-century pauper entered into the twentieth century, where the economic turf permits no handicappers. You can find him in Cleveland, in Buffalo, in Pittsburgh, and in Chicago, where 27 percent of all the city's Negroes are on the welfare rolls. He is part of the new poverty.

The second addition to the impoverished of the sixties also is a relatively new American. Maybe he will add a new work to the Labor Department's classifications of "unskilled," "semiskilled," and "skilled." For he is the "deskilled" American.

He is the individual who once did a task well, only to watch the need for that task disappear. And it was a specific task to which he had devoted all his energies. It might have been in a mine shaft in West Virginia, in a packing plant in Chicago, at an open-hearth furnace in Buffalo or Cleveland. But the deskilled are not confined to the sweat-and-muscle laborers. Donald Michael, in *Cybernation: the Silent Conquest,* has shown the inroads the machine has made and will continue to make on white-collar workers.

But if the new poor are largely unknown to most Americans, so, frequently, is the source from which they may obtain help. I once thought that the dollars I contributed to the United Fund campaign were spent to help the orphans, the poor unfortunate family, or someone who was simply down on his luck. And when my newspaper published the large expenditures made for public welfare, I, like so many others, was a little annoyed, because I thought that my charity dollars had already done that job. I am afraid there are many Americans who still have the same impression.

I know now, as social workers do, that this is not the case. We know that the problems of poverty today have the stamp of government property all over them. . . .

. . .

. . . I am a bit surprised, for example, that one of the largest private agencies, with local representation throughout the United States, today finds that fewer than half of its clients are in the lower class. I am surprised, too, that the majority of its customers in this class never reach a second interview.

Even where private charity is involved directly with the poor, frequently much of the cost of that involvement is paid by the government. For example, I was surprised to learn that in my own state, New York, for example, of $57 million spent in 1961 by private institutions for children and by child-caring agencies, $42 million came from the taxpayers. I wonder if most people realize this.

From these developments we see that we not only have a new poor but an expanding provider as well. And that major provider, called "government," for some curious reason has long been considered by most Americans as an anathema second only to the mother-in-law problem.

. . .

. . . If in the sixties we have a new poor and, we hope, a new politician, I think we also have a new collection of ladies and gentlemen who have "clout" and, if you will, "drag."

Social work's many endeavors had their beginnings with the help of the power structure, with the help of the decision-makers. These were, by and large, the elite, whose names graced the social register, who in some communities could be counted on a very few hands, and in New York once were confined to the arbitrary figure of 400. The generosity of these Brahmins is still evident today, but they are no longer the sole decision-makers. Theirs are no longer the names that a man who knows his community would offer if you asked him: Who runs this town?

I think this may be the key lesson learned from our public welfare project. This project was conducted by the State Charities Aid Association of New York, a ninety-one-year-old private agency of citizens interested in health and welfare programs, and was supported by a Field Foundation grant. It brought those who run the town directly in touch with those who live on the awkward side of the railroad tracks.

What we learned was that the list of those—the decision-makers—who have the "clout" in most communities included too many names that were not on the boards or committees of social agencies which deal with the social problems of those communities. Our list of "important" people disagreed with theirs.

The project confronted both politics and power with poverty. I say "confront," but in some instances the participants described the meeting as a "collision." This project was a small attempt to show industrial, political, civic, and union leaders poverty as it exists—not by talking about it, not by viewing with alarm, not by writing about it, and not by distributing pamphlets or brochures.

In ten cities we took the community leadership into the slums. Each participant spent an afternoon with a welfare department caseworker and accompanied him into the homes of general relief and ADC families. The caseworkers showed them a cross section of the families who were dependent upon the tax dollar for their support.

Our participants were shielded from nothing. They saw the rat- and vermin-infested hovels for which they, as taxpayers, were paying such high rent. They saw firsthand the problems of illegitimacy. They saw firsthand a mother trying to provide for her brood on an ADC budget. And they saw, too, dirt, indifference, and the individual shortcomings that are part of public welfare.

. . .

At the end of the afternoon of visits, when the participants joined us for dinner and a discussion of what they had seen, the group of industrialists and politicians sounded like beginning caseworkers. For once there was a sense of identification with poverty. Expressions like "my family," "my caseworker," and "this child that I saw in this place" were used.

We did not stumble on any magic formula. We did not produce any wholesale change of heart. What we did do, though, was to induce awareness and concern, two of the first necessities if poverty is ever to be understood. Here are three excerpts from the many comments made by our participants:

An editor said: "The experiences of the day contributed to a sleepless night and a realization that answers must be found that are neither glib rationalizations nor stereotyped defenses either of the pro or con sides."

The president of one of this nation's major corporations, with plants scattered throughout the world, said: "Although my schedule is exceedingly crowded, I am very glad that I took the time to participate. Contrary to my experience in most situations, I came back without any convictions on how the problem can be solved."

A League of Women Voters president said: "If your purpose was to provoke a new and different interest in public welfare problems, you have succeeded admirably."

The individuals who took part in the project were, we believed, among the major forces in their communities. As you see, however, they differ in a number of instances from the listing that one would take from the social register. They included: six mayors; thirteen county executives or chairmen of boards of supervisors; six state legislators; thirteen newspaper editors; seventeen corporation executives; nine presidents of chapters of the League of Women Voters; three heads of labor councils; and eight heads of taxpayer groups or chambers of commerce.

For many of these men and women this was their first real contact with the problems of poverty, even though some of them had made lengthy speeches about the subject. A few may have had a connection with the United Fund campaign or the Boy Scouts, and, in several cases, with a community welfare council. Yet their daily sphere of influence and, in some instances, their decisions directly affect the degree of progress or of stagnation in solving the social problems in their communities.

There was without doubt a noticeable difference between the supposed power structure of the board members of social agencies and the participants in our project. Because this difference exists, and because the relatively new decision-makers have been on the outside, or at best, on the periphery of the poverty problem, the difficulties we face today have been further complicated. If I may generalize, I do not think that the new leaders have met the new poor.

. . .

We must spend a great deal of time showing Americans who are "the new poor." We must bury the old images of an impoverished middle class. And I offer as a small and certainly not conclusive cure the project with which we have been experimenting. I think it can help to *show* leading

Americans who some of the poor are; for they must be shown as well as told.

This is vital if we ever are to reach what the Military calls "an overview" about poverty today. Once influential Americans know who the poor are, they will begin to realize that public welfare is not just another expensive government function, but that it is the funnel of failure for a variety of other community endeavors.

It is then they will see that a race riot in Birmingham—a riot prompted in part by lack of job opportunities—may have something to do with the relief problems of Cleveland, of Chicago, or of Pittsburgh, if job opportunities do not exist there either.

Secondly, let us look at power. We need to incorporate the men and women who are now among the missing into the social problems of our communities. . . .

We must make room for the local union leader, for the plant manager, and even for the local spokesman of the Tax-payers League or the Chamber of Commerce. Years of per-sistent opposition from some of these people has gained social welfare precious little. It is time to try another approach.

There is a bridge between the terrain of politics and the one we have called "power." It is time, too, that the politician, be he a mayor, the state legislator, or a congressman, not be invited to speak at an annual meeting, but be urged, even pressured, to become a working member of some of these agencies—or at least of a community welfare council. . . .

(12)

Work, Family, and Community in a Rural Depressed Area

ROBERT PERRUCCI AND
KICHIRO K. IWAMOTO

Many rural areas in the United States are chronic low-income areas with high rates of unemployment and under-employment. The far-reaching technological, occupational and educational changes of the last fifty years have left these areas with a larger supply of human resources in relation to the land and capital resources necessary to maintain a decent level of living. The reduction in forms and farm occupations has resulted in large numbers of unemployed who are un-suited for non-farm occupations. In many cases out-migration of the younger, better educated individuals in these areas has left behind a population less able to adapt to the demands of a rapidly changing society. The plight of these rural areas is well known, but too often the problem has been described in terms of the rates of unemployment. More recently the problem has been brought into sharper focus by the recognition in public policy of the needs of the under-employed. The Manpower Development and Training Act of 1962 has explicitly equated underemployment with unem-ployment stating that "workers in farm families with less than $1200 annual net income shall be considered unem-ployed for the purpose of this act."

§ The authors thank the Purdue Research Foundation and Purdue Agricultural Experiment Station for their support of the larger project from which this paper, previously unpublished, was drawn.

Numerous remedies have been offered to ease the economic situation of low-income areas. One class of such remedies is focused upon the incorporation of additional resources into the area as well as a more intensive and "rational" use of existing resources. Many of these solutions are limited by the fact that farms in low-income areas operate with such restricted resources that the usual farm programs have little effect upon the incomes of these farm families. Similarly, programs designed to lead to the adoption of new technology, better farm practices, and management require educational programs that will facilitate the adoption of innovations and a population that will be receptive to these educational programs.

Another class of solutions has to do with encouraging and facilitating movement into other jobs and areas by low-income area residents. Here again there are problems related to the desirability and effectiveness of such solutions. First of all, we would need to know something of the existing skills and abilities of those persons seeking new employment. In order for job mobility to be a feasible solution for the unemployed and underemployed there must be a sensible fit between the occupations in the labor market and the skills and training of persons available to fill these occupations. Since persons in rural low-income areas who need employment are most likely to be unskilled farm laborers, there are severe restrictions on the likelihood that they can find a place in the labor market. Even if unskilled non-farm occupations are available for the unemployed and underemployed in low-income areas these are jobs which have their own form of instability and insecurity. The ultimate effect of such job changes might simply be that the unemployment is transferred from the rural area to the city.

Thus we have a large number of adults in low-income rural areas who do not possess the education and skills necessary to obtain employment in stable non-farm occupations. In order to get to areas of greater employment opportunities, programs are needed for the education and guidance of young people in the secondary schools as well as adult education and training programs. Retraining programs, however, have indicated that while they can be effective, they can also be costly, time consuming, and limited in their coverage.

This brings us to the consideration of factors that will be the central focus of the remainder of this paper. Here we will be concerned with the individual, social and cultural factors that induce or constrain a person in a rural depressed area to accept or reject the possibility of undertaking a job change and a community change. The basic framework we shall follow assumes that a person in a low-income area is faced with the possibility of a decision to take a new job and to select a new community in which to live. Each of these decisions may be seen as dependent upon the following: (a) a person's attachment to his community; (b) attachments to his family and kinship group; (c) attachments to his job and knowledge of alternative jobs; and (d) a person's values and aspirations.

This framework was explored in a pilot study of a rural low-income county in the midwest which we shall call Hill County. An interdisciplinary team sought (1) to examine the social and cultural factors affecting mobility; (2) to determine the available skills and potential retrainability of persons in the county; and (3) to estimate existing employment opportunities and potential future needs within the county. The data discussed in this paper were collected from a sample of approximately 200 residents of Hill County.

Hill County: Economy and Population

Following the pattern of most low-income rural areas, Hill County has had a steady loss of population. The population, which has historically been white and born within the state (less than one per cent non-white and ten per cent born outside the state), has shown a steady decline since 1900. There has been an average population decrease of about seven per cent per decade, with a decline from 13,476 residents in 1900 to 8,379 residents in 1960.

The differential migration rates by age and sex have left

Hill County with a large proportion of older people. For males, the age groups of 5–14, 15–24, and 25–34 have shown the greatest decline in population. This pattern appears to be the response to a precarious labor market which has forced many persons to migrate out of the county in order to find employment. The declining pre-labor market age group (5–15) combined with the migration of persons in the labor market age groups, suggests a continued and perhaps more rapid decline in the county's population. This prospective pattern is further supported by the female population losses in the age groups 5–14 and 15–24, the latter being the greatest single loss category for women.

In addition to the high out-migration from this low-income area, there has not been a very satisfactory level of employment for those persons who chose to remain in the county. During 1962 more than one-third of the male labor force in Hill County between the ages of 16–55 experienced some unemployment. The unemployment rates were found to be highest in the younger and the older age groups.

These unemployment and underemployment rates have combined to produce the lowest median family income of any county in the state. The seriousness of these employment figures, in terms of human problems, is reflected in the very limited unemployment insurance coverage available to persons in the county. Of the 2600 persons in Hill County listed as employed in the 1960 census reports, only 274 workers were in covered employment on unemployment insurance benefits. Thus persons in low-income rural areas suffer not only from high rates of unemployment and underemployment, but also from the absence of protection in periods of economic strife.

Now let us turn to a closer look at the residents of Hill County. What are their values, aspirations, kinship and community ties? How are these characteristics related to the likelihood that unemployed and underemployed persons would be willing to undertake retraining programs that would result in job changes and area changes? These questions indicate that the problems of low-income areas cannot be solved simply by providing retraining or creating new jobs. Changing jobs and moving to a new community involve much more than learning a new set of skills. Our interviews with Hill County residents can begin to provide some answers to these important questions.

Work and Aspirations

Of the approximately 200 Hill County residents who were interviewed, about one-quarter were in white collar occupations ranging from professional to clerical and sales positions, the larger number being in clerical and sales and minor professional positions. The other three-quarters were in agricultural and blue collar occupations. Compared to the occupations of their fathers, our respondents showed a certain amount of occupational inheritance and occupational mobility. Of those whose fathers were in white collar occupations, about 60 per cent were also in white collar occupations. Among sons of fathers in blue collar occupations, the amount of occupational inheritance was of the order of 85 per cent. As might be expected, sons of fathers who were in agriculture had the lowest rates of occupational inheritance, generally moving out of agriculture into blue collar positions. These patterns of mobility and immobility reveal quite clearly the restricted nature of the opportunity structure in a rural low-income area.

Looking only at occupational inheritance in farm occupations for our younger and older respondents, we find, as expected, that the older sons of farmers are more likely to have followed in their father's footsteps than the younger sons of fathers who were farmers.

What do these rather high rates of occupational inheritance, especially among blue collar workers, tell us about workers and the meaning of work in a low-income rural area? Do such patterns indicate a traditional orientation among our respondents, an orientation that would result in a low level of occupational aspiration? Or are such patterns of inheritance simply the natural response to a limited opportunity structure in terms of available alternatives, which is perhaps combined with traditionalistic commitments toward the family and the community? We attempted to explore these questions by asking our respondents about their work satisfactions and their general plans and aspirations.

When asked about satisfaction with their work, a little more than eight out of ten of the respondents indicated that they were satisfied with their occupation. A higher proportion of the white collar than the blue collar worker indicated satisfaction, but the differences were not large enough to be important. Given the poor economic conditions in the county it is perhaps surprising to find such a high proportion of persons expressing satisfaction with their occupation. It is possible, however, that the absence of available alternatives has the result of enhancing a person's evaluation of his present occupation. This possibility was borne out by the fact that when our respondents were asked about jobs in Hill County, fewer than one out of ten had knowledge of job opportunities in the county.

Another approach to job satisfaction is to examine whether a person would undertake a different occupation if given the opportunity. When we asked our respondents about their desire for a different line of work we got a different picture of job satisfaction. More than sixty per cent of our blue collar workers wished that they were in a different line of work, as compared to thirty per cent of the white collar workers. This suggests that at least our blue collar respondents might be amenable to a new occupation if one was available.

An attempt was made to examine the level of aspiration of our subjects in the hope of separating the individual motivational level from what might only be a response to a set of objective constraints. There are two aspects of aspiration level with which we are concerned: a future orientation and a risk orientation. In attempting to measure future orientation we asked our sample several questions dealing with future plans and prospects. When asked about their chances of getting ahead socially and economically, 21 per cent of the white collar workers and 7 per cent of the blue collar workers thought they were excellent. The remaining respondents in each occupational group saw their chances for advancement as being fair to limited. A similar question posed to the respondents concerned the extent to which they had any definite plans for the future. Among the white collar respondents, 43 per cent had definite plans for the future, while 20 per cent of the blue collar workers had such plans.

In attempting to ascertain risk orientation, which we felt to be a component of a high level of aspiration, each subject was asked to choose the most desirable of three occupations varying in risk and reward; one occupation offering a moderate income but being very secure; the second having a good income but having a higher risk element; and the third occupation with a very high income but a very high risk of losing it. Among the white collar respondents the percentages choosing each occupation respectively were 47 per cent, 24 per cent, and 28 per cent. The distribution for the blue collar workers was 68 per cent, 18 per cent, and 14 per cent.

Thus it appears that our blue collar respondents have fewer crystallized plans for the future and are more security oriented with respect to occupational choice, undoubtedly influenced by a combination of lack of stability of their present jobs and the economic plight of the county. What effect these two individual qualities have upon the likelihood that persons in low-income areas will seek to better their economic condition may depend upon the views held of the two major means for advancement in our society, education and work. Some findings concerning the importance of education and work for rural area residents have been obtained in a number of other studies. One study of attitudes and values in a rural area, suggests that work is not valued highly, and that education, while necessary, is not seen as requiring any sacrifice in order to be obtained. Another study, a comparison of educational aspirations among 10th and 12th grade boys, found that educational aspirations declined across the following groups: urban, small-town, rural non-farm, and farm. Even more important, perhaps, is the fact that parents of farm boys offered more discouragement than encouragement with respect to education.

An attempt was made to ascertain attitudes toward work and education among Hill County residents. It was found that attitudes toward work and education are significantly related to occupation, employment status, education, and a number of aptitude scales such as verbal ability and numerical ability. These patterns would suggest that the Hill County residents who are most in need of a job retraining program (at least from an economic point of view) may not be entirely receptive to attempts to obtain their participation in such programs. Again it suggests the need for a broader-based community program which goes beyond job retraining to include an understanding of both the individual and community problems of low-income areas.

Family and Community Ties

Undertaking a new job or moving to a new community is a much more far reaching decision to our Hill County respondents than a simple calculation of relative advantage in economic gains and losses. A man's work is more than a source of income; it also represents a pattern of established relationships to friends and to family alike. In much the same way, the community can be a basic source of satisfaction for a person, the setting within which he is known and in turn knows others. Family, friends and community ties can serve as powerful negative sources of motivation for the person considering a new job and a new community.

Since most Hill County residents were born in the county and have spent their entire lives there, it should not be too surprising to find an elaborate family system among our respondents. Each person was asked to indicate the number of immediate relatives (parents and siblings), and the total number of relatives (aunts, uncles, cousins, etc.) that lived within a 50-mile radius of his home. A little more than 40 per cent of the white collar workers had fewer than four immediate relatives living in the area, 37 per cent had five or six relatives, and the remaining 20 per cent had more than seven immediate relatives in the area. The blue collar respondents had a slightly different pattern with respect to relatives. About 43 per cent of the blue collar workers had fewer than four immediate family relatives in the area, 15 per cent had five or six relatives, and the remaining 42 per cent had more than seven relatives in the area.

These figures indicate that a number of family members are located in close enough proximity to have potentially important effects upon an individual's decision to leave the county. However, if we look at the total number of relatives living in a 50-mile radius, the number of possible binding social relationships is quite overwhelming. Over 50 per cent of our white collar respondents had more than twenty-one relatives living within a 50-mile radius of their homes, with over a third of these having more than thirty-six relatives within this distance. Looking at the blue collar respondents we find that a little less than half had twenty-one or more relatives in the area, with just under one-half of these having more than thirty-six relatives.

It is also apparently much more than the sheer proximity of relatives that is important here; for when asked about the frequency with which they see their relatives, over half of both the blue collar and white collar respondents indicated that they see their relatives once a week or more. The significance of these extensive kinship connections goes beyond the mere emotional ties that they provide, although these are certainly important. Under conditions of economic uncertainty, which is certainly prevalent among our Hill County residents, the existence of so many relatives can function as networks of self-help patterns among family members. Moving to a new area may mean losing not only emotional support but also economic support as well.

Looking at community ties as another factor which may serve to influence the decision to move to a new community, we find that participation in voluntary associations is significantly higher than the national rural rate. Among our sample we found that 75 per cent of the residents belong to at least one organization, while the national equivalent rate is 41 per cent. In terms of active participation, 65 per cent of the respondents regularly participate in one or more weekly organizational activities. This high rate of active participation is reinforced by the community activities of the spouses of our respondents, with about 15 per cent of the wives of white collar workers participating in formal associations three or more times a week, and 25 per cent of the wives of blue collar workers being similarly active. Oddly enough, the spouses of our respondents had lower rates of informal friendship and visiting patterns (outside of the family relations) than they had with respect to formal participation. About 15 per cent of the white collar spouses are involved in informal activities at least twice a week as compared to 6 per cent of the blue collar spouses.

The general pattern of family and community ties as suggested by our data indicates an elaborate network of structural connections to people and organizations in Hill County. Such patterns are to be expected when considering the general geographical immobility of our sample. Over 70 per cent of them have lived in Hill County at least twenty years, and about half of the respondents have not had a residential change within the county in the last ten years. One may expect that these family and community connections are strong, and of importance to the residents. Attempts to encourage voluntary migration will have to take these ties into consideration.

Final Notes on Mobility and Migration

The central concern of this paper was to examine the social and cultural factors which may aid or inhibit the decision to undertake a new job and to move to a new community among residents in a rural low-income area. A central assumption was that both mobility and migration were possible solutions to the problem of unemployment and underemployment in these areas. However the solution to these economic problems goes beyond the retraining of the unemployed and underemployed and assuming that they will take new jobs in new communities. An ameliorative program such as this attempts to induce and encourage voluntary mobility and migration. The main problem is one of implementing such a program without making it too coercive by replacing free choice with compulsion. While seeking economic betterment for the individual, community and the nation, we must maintain an understanding for the emotional investments a man may make in a way of life that is partly symbolized by his work, family and community.

Maintaining an understanding for the many problems associated with mobility and migration can be institutionalized by infusing community organizations such as schools with these essential ideas. Schools must continue to orient their vocational programs to national and regional rather than local markets. They must also provide students with information and programs that will enable them to make wiser educational and career decisions. Only with effective education can we get free choice and free movement in the labor market and still get an effective distribution of our manpower.

An even more important innovation, from the point of view of the human problems involved, is the creation of community organizations that will aid the transition process from rural to urban area. Along with new skills and new jobs, we need new understanding of the patterns of life in low-income areas and the many problems involved in the seemingly straightforward decision to take a new job.

THE CULTURE OF
POVERTY

T HE *"culture" of poverty is a relatively new concept, coined probably by Oscar Lewis in his book* Children of Sanchez. *It is widely accepted today to describe the ways of life of the poor in the habitats of the poor. However, it is not uncontested. We bring first an excerpt from a scholarly article by Elizabeth Herzog, Director of Child Life Studies Branch, Department of Health, Education, and Welfare, in which she discusses the basis for the assumption of the culture concept of poverty as it is reflected in the publications and investigations of numerous authors (page 92). The article is followed by a number of case studies of urban and rural ways of the life of the poor. The excerpts from the "Puerto Ricans in New York," and "Chicago's Hillbilly Ghetto" (page 103), show the plight and difficulties of recent "immigrants" to big city living. They share the heritage of desolate poverty with the Negro in West Harlem on 114th Street (page 115). Paul Jacobs describes in "Man With a Hoe" the hard, insecure, resigned life of a farm day laborer (page 117). "The Outskirts of Hope" pictures the helpless, fearful attitude of an unemployed worker in the Appalachian mountains when he is confronted with the ways of modern bureaucracies. The author, Mary Wright, a social case worker in the region, with an unusual gift for observing and understanding her clients, writes what she sees and experiences (page 125).*

⟦ 13 ⟧

Is There a Culture of Poverty?

ELIZABETH HERZOG

. . . Oscar Lewis summarized succinctly the reasons for believing that there is a culture of poverty, when he said:

> In anthropological usage, the term culture implies, essentially, a design for living which is passed down from generation to generation. In applying this concept of culture to the understanding of poverty, I want to draw attention to the fact that poverty in modern nations is not only a state of economic deprivation, of disorganization, or of the absence of something. It is also something positive in the sense that it has a structure, a rationale, and defense mechanisms without which the poor could hardly carry on. In short, it is a way of life, remarkably stable and persistent, passed down from generation to generation along family lines. The culture of poverty has its own modalities and distinctive social and psychological consequences for its members. (From *Children of Sanchez.*)

He was talking about a culture of poverty that cuts across national borders, including those of the United States, to which the present comments are confined. Our first question concerns his thesis: Is there a culture of poverty?

One way to approach this question is to list a number of traits or characteristics attributed to the poor by different investigators and supported at least to some degree by evidence. The summary given below is by no means exhaustive.

§ Adapted from Elizabeth Herzog, "Some Assumptions About the Poor," *Social Service Review,* vol. 37, December 1963, pp. 391–400 (copyright © 1963 by The University of Chicago), by permission of The University of Chicago Press.

It does not include all the traits or characteristics attributed with supporting evidence. But none which is mentioned has been put forward without some supporting evidence, even though the quality and quantity of the evidence may have been far from conclusive.

The poor, by definition, are described as having little money, virtually no savings, no economic security. This means, among other things, buying often and in small amounts—and getting less for their money than do the rich. . . .

Poverty involves underemployment and scattered, irregular, miscellaneous employment, often at undesirable occupations; it involves extensive borrowing through formal and informal sources, use of second-hand clothing and furniture, and overcrowded dwellings and lack of privacy. The poor have a higher death rate, a lower life expectancy, lower levels of health—physical and mental—and of nutrition, than the prosperous; they depend more on home remedies and folk medicine, since medical care is expensive and frightening; they are relatively unlikely to be members of labor unions, political parties, and other organizations; they are more inclined to excessive drinking and to violence than the prosperous.

These are familiar variables. Equally familiar is the inverse relation of education and income, the fact that education has been, at least until recently, the most useful single indicator of socioeconomic status. Sometimes it almost seems as if all the other differences flowed from that one, so overwhelming are its apparent results in the lives and thoughts and feelings of the poor. Associated with low education are low school achievement, inadequate verbal skills, lack of intellectual stimulation, lack of motivation to education—often coupled with unrealistic aspirations and unrealistic faith in education as an open sesame to getting on in the world. . . .

Psychological Characteristics Associated with Poverty

Less obvious, but nevertheless supported by empirical evidence, are certain psychological characteristics attributed to the poor. A number of investigators have presented evidence to show that the poor tend on the whole to be more authoritarian than the prosperous; more given to intolerance and prejudice; more given to black-and-white thinking; more anti-intellectual; more prone to action and less contemplation; more inclined to personal and concrete rather than impersonal and abstract thinking; more given to resignation and fatalism; more subject to anomie; more inclined to a concrete and magical emphasis in religion; more provincial and locally oriented in attitudes and opinions; more distrustful of governmental authority; more suspicious and hostile toward the police; less developed in imaginative and logical powers; more given to economic liberalism and more reactionary in non-economic matters; less eager to preserve civil liberties, if they themselves are not members of a minority group.

We are told, too, that among the poor we find more hostility, more tension, and more aggression than among those who live well above the subsistence level. One report comments that, in encouraging their children to fight back, these mothers show a realistic understanding of the social problems in their neighborhoods. This view receives support from a low-income father who said of his son: "I . . . knock the hell out of him, 'cause he can't be no sissy and grow up in this here jungle."

Two other generalizations are often made and seldom challenged . . . . One is that the poor have less belief in their control over their own destinies than the prosperous—less sense of autonomy. The other is that their time perspective is shorter, that they are present-oriented rather than future-oriented.

This is an incomplete list of various kinds of attributes that have been mentioned as differentiating the very poor from the more prosperous. They are listed here chiefly as background for considering the usefulness of that currently popular phrase, the culture of poverty.

. . .

Lack of a distinctive technology and possibly of art forms constitutes a real but trivial defect in the concept of a culture of poverty. More substantial is the lack of the basic core that gives to a culture its identity as a culture: the sense that its members have a belonging to a culture entity with its institutions, patterns, and shared beliefs; a sense of that entity as good—a sense of allegiance as well as of identity. There are cultures whose members want to break away, but if they do break away at least they have the feeling that they are separating themselves from an entity that exists and that claims them as members. Corollary to this is the sense of sharing and participating in the life of a broad group, of sharing in a system of beliefs and practices. This positive aspect of culture, the sense of belonging, with its corollary elements of sharing and of participating, seems to be absent from the so-called culture of poverty.

Some of the closest students of slum life emphasize the unincorporated quality of the individuals who make up the slums. There are gangs and cliques composed of some members; but the neighborhoods, they say, consist of people who happen to live near each other. The lack of worldly goods, according to these observers of large city slums, does not create a sense of community, of common institutions and customs, practices and beliefs.

The few people who challenge the idea of a culture of poverty assert that in great cities the poor live relatively isolated lives; that, as Disraeli said, "there is aggregation, but aggregation under circumstances which make it rather a dissociating than a uniting principle," and that the life-ways of the slum dwellers represent, not a system of culturally evolved patterns, but rather a series of disjoined pragmatic adjustments to exigencies perceived as unpredictable and uncontrollable.

These represent the chief qualifications to the concept of culture applied to the poor. They do not destroy the usefulness of the concept, provided its limits are recognized. They do, however, reduce the usefulness if these limits are not recognized, for failure to recognize them invites a neostereotyping, which in turn invites distortion and misapprehension.

. . . The culture of poverty should be thought of as a sub-culture rather than as a culture in itself. . . .

Whether we call it a culture or a subculture, it is always important to avoid the cookie-cutter view of culture, with regard to the individual and to the culture or subculture involved. With regard to the individual, the cookie-cutter view assumes that all individuals in a culture turn out exactly alike, as if they were so many cookies. It overlooks the fact that, at least in our urban society, every individual is a member of more than one subculture; and which subculture most strongly influences his response in a given situation depends on the interaction of a great many factors, including his individual make-up and history, the specifics of the various subcultures to which he belongs, and the specifics of the given situation. Thus, although we find prevailing regularities in what might be called culture-character and behavior, and although it is highly useful to recognize these regularities, it is also useful to remember the vast range of individual differences that coexist with these prevailing patterns of thought, feeling, and behavior.

With regard to the culture as a whole, the cookie-cutter concept again assumes a spurious homogeneity. It forgets that within any one culture or subculture there are conflicts and contradictions and that at any given moment an individual may have to choose—consciously or unconsciously—between conflicting values or patterns. . . .

. . . Also, most individuals, in varying degrees, have a dual set of values—those by which they live and those they cherish as best. . . . This point—duality of values—has been made and documented repeatedly about the culture of poverty. The poor . . . to a large extent accept and believe in the standards and values of the middle class, but many of the poor regard those standards as a luxury appropriate only to those who can afford it—like a yacht or a mink coat. And so it is possible, without too much discomfort, to behave as if these standards did not exist and at the same time to prefer those standards to one's own behavior. . . .

In the view of this writer the culture of poverty is a very

useful concept, if and only if it is used with discrimination, with recognition that poverty is a subculture, and with avoidance of the cookie-cutter approach. It should be added that these provisos have been met by the investigators most responsible for giving it currency. . . .

FAMILY STRUCTURE AND SEX PATTERNS ASSOCIATED WITH POVERTY

Our second statement is that the family structure and sex patterns of the poor differ from those of the non-poor. There is a good deal of empirical evidence for this statement. There is evidence that not only separation and desertion but also divorce vary in frequency in inverse proportion to income and that family size also varies inversely with income. There is evidence, too, that families headed by women are far more frequent among the poor than among the prosperous and that births out of wedlock are also far more frequent among the poor. There is evidence that child-rearing practices differ, with physical punishment and ridicule being more frequent as one descends the social-economic scale. . . . Although a number could be added, these seem enough to justify accepting the second assumption—namely, that the family and sex patterns of the poor differ from those of the middle class.

This does not, of course, tell much about how they differ. When one gets into that question, one is bound to become involved in our third statement. Accordingly, it seems simpler to consider them together. The third is: The family and sex patterns of poor Negroes differ from those of whites on the same socioeconomic level.

One of the big obstacles to assessing that statement is the fact, mentioned before, that adequate controlling of socio-economic factors is rarely found. . . .

We find that some reports of differences in Negro and white family and sex patterns are based on inadequate matching. This does not mean that there are no differences, but merely that these particular studies have failed to document the existence of differences. In each of these studies, it happened that the patterns usually ascribed to lower socioeconomic levels were stronger among the Negroes than among the whites.

A different kind of evidence comes from studies of available figures on marital stability and on fertility. Thomas Monahan, after careful analysis of statistics on divorce and on premarital pregnancy, came to the conclusion that there is higher incidence of divorce among Negroes than among whites, even when socioeconomic factors are controlled, but that the slavery-legacy theory is probably not tenable. Some others report that the differences seem wholly attributable to socioeconomic factors. Our National Vital Statistics Division reports fertility rates much higher among non-whites than among whites—a finding generally accepted and often referred to. On the other hand, a fairly recent review of information on differential fertility, although it underwrites the familiar belief that fertility rates rise as one descends the socioeconomic scale, adds that when socioeconomic factors are controlled the alleged higher fertility rates among Negroes are revealed to relate to the socioeconomic status rather than to race. These are two very different kinds of variables, though they both relate to the color-versus-class question.

A few other researchers have tried to compare both by socioeconomic indexes and by color. Clark Vincent has attempted this in his studies of unmarried mothers, as have Jones, Meyer, Borgatta, and others. The findings here showed that both color and socioeconomic status exerted an influence, but that the influence of socioeconomic status was considerably stronger. The studies are few enough and limited enough to cause one to want more evidence. Nevertheless they are encouraging steps in the direction of learning what we need to know.

A different group of studies is relevant here—namely, poverty studies that deal entirely or predominantly with white subjects. Again and again one reads descriptions of the lower class that sound exactly like patterns often ascribed to lower-lower Negroes—and often . . . ascribed to the heritage of

slavery. *Plainville, U.S.A.* describes the group referred to by
the citizenry as "people who live like animals." No mention is
made of color, but it is clear that those described are white.
The same can be said of the lower-lower class described by
Hollingshead, Warner, and others.

Finally, there are some investigators who have studied both
Negroes and whites and who (so far) report no substantial
differences in family and sex patterns at the same socioeconomic level. Walter Miller is one of these. The published
accounts of his Roxbury study reviewed so far do not make a
point of differentiating between white and non-white; but in
discussion he has been emphatic in the conviction that the
patterns he describes are related to socioeconomic rather than
to ethnic characteristics. . . .

Oscar Lewis, in describing what he means by the culture
of poverty, lists some family characteristics that he ascribes
to poverty in any urban Western society. He includes a trend
toward mother-centered families, a relatively high incidence
of the abandonment of mothers and children, a belief in male
superiority with an accompanying cult of masculinity, frequent resort to violence in the settlement of quarrels, frequent
use of physical punishment in the training of children, wife-
beating, early initiation into sex, free unions, or consensual
marriages. All of these characteristics are found in studies of
our urban poor, whether white or Negro.

THREE "MARITAL AXIOMS"

. . . From the Washington study of low-income families
directed by Hylan Lewis . . . emerge three propositions
about marriage that seem to be regarded as axiomatic among
the very poor. Available evidence suggests that the following
three "marital axioms" represent points of convergence rather
than differences between family and sex patterns among low-
income whites and non-whites.

The first is that a good marriage is far better than no marriage. The second is that a bad marriage is far worse than no

marriage. The third is that for a girl to bear a child out of wedlock is unfortunate, but does not necessarily impair her chances for a good marriage.

The positive value put on a good marriage and the negative value put on illegitimacy have escaped a number of observers, because both differ from those found in the middle class. The social and psychological plus of a good marriage is extremely high. The negative value of birth out of wedlock, for mother and for child, although it exists, is not nearly so strong. Moreover, neither marriage nor birth out of wedlock stands as high on the value pyramid of the poor as do a number of other values. They are important, but not the most important.

All the mothers interviewed in the Washington study, white and non-white, were asked at some point how they would feel if a daughter of theirs became pregnant out of wedlock. The answer was unanimous: they would feel terrible. It would be pain and grief. "That's why I always prayed for boys," one mother said. But they were almost as unanimous in declaring that they would not urge the prospective parents to marry unless they really loved each other. "An unhappy marriage," they agree, "is worse than no marriage at all." But a good marriage is important. . . .

Attitudes toward both marriage and illegitimacy are obviously interwoven with many other ingredients of that deceptively simple phrase, family and sex patterns. Two that must be mentioned are the war between the sexes and the cult of masculinity. . . .

There seems no doubt that the lower one goes on the social-economic ladder, the more overt and bitter becomes the war between the sexes. It seems clear also that this generalization cuts across the color line. . . .

Add to this the fact that the men feel dominant and the women feel downtrodden. Such a statement is at odds with the frequent assertions that, because Negro women are more able to get and hold jobs, they have the upper hand opposite Negro men. The men are indeed at a disadvantage, economically, and the ramifications are infinite. However, this does not mean that the women have things their own way. If the women are the dominant sex among low-income Negroes, the women do not know it. On that score, one of them remarked, "I've often heard a woman wish she was a man, but I never heard a man wish he was a woman."

If most men are beasts and most women are exploited by them, then a smart woman does not want marriage unless she can find that rare paragon, a really good husband. If she can find him, then she is successful. If she bears a child out of wedlock, that is a social misfortune. But illegitimate children do not necessarily preclude a good marriage, and lack of marriage does not necessarily preclude sex.

There may be differences in the degree and expression of the sex war and the cult of masculine superiority among Negroes and whites on the lowest socioeconomic level. Nevertheless, the similarities are striking.

With regard to the whole complex of family and sex patterns, one may say the same thing. Whether there are differences, and, if so, what they are, remains a question. On the basis of this somewhat telescoped discussion it seems reasonable to conclude two things: that the differences related to color, if they exist at all, are probably far slighter than has often been assumed; and that we do not yet have the kind of evidence that would give adequate basis for a firm conclusion on the matter.

It may be added, as a speculation, that there probably are some differences related to ethnic background, but that probably they are dwarfed by the similarities related to socioeconomic status. One cluster of reasons for thinking that some differences do exist has to do with the special status of Negro Americans today, including their history, their current situation, and the continuing struggle against discrimination being waged for them and by them. Another reason is based on the many discriminations that—to our shame and our regret— still exist. Analysis of aid to dependent children caseloads in one state showed more abuse and neglect of children among whites than among Negroes and "a higher proportion of white cases in which parents are deteriorated, with severe personality disturbances making it impossible for them to be

adequate parents." Such a report suggests that the white
people found on the lowest socioeconomic levels may be, on
the average, less capable and more disturbed than the Negroes
on this level. If so, it is probably because social and economic
conditions make it easier for white people to rise from
poverty, so that for them the screening process is more
directly related to basic competence. In order to remain one
of the poor, a Negro does not have to have something wrong
with him. The speculation about prevailing likenesses and
differences, however, remains speculative. . . .

〖 14 〗

Chicago's Hillbilly Ghetto

HAL BRUNO

The plight of the Southern Negroes who move North in
vain search of the Promised Land is well known these days.
Their difficulties have tended to obscure the fact that during
the postwar years increasing numbers of poor white families
from the South have also been migrating to the industrial
North, where they too have yet to be absorbed into the fabric
of big-city life. Known to social workers as "Southern white
Appalachian migrants," they remain isolated in the squalor of
Anglo-Saxon ghettos.

Hard times drive them North in search of jobs as the coal
mines shut down, factories automate, and marginal farms
collapse in debt. So they pile into rattletrap cars and arrive

§ Hal Bruno, "Chicago's Hillbilly Ghetto," reprinted from *The Reporter*, vol. 30, no. 12, June 4, 1964, pp. 28–31 (copyright © 1964 by
The Reporter Magazine Company), by permission of publisher and
author.

in places like Chicago with no training to compete in the job market and no preparation to make the difficult transition from rural to urban living. In the city, the Southern whites become the victims of old slum problems while creating some new ones. They are undernourished, uneducated, unwanted, and unable to cope with a society that does not understand them or their ways. Lacking leadership, organization, or political power, these descendants of the pioneers are a lost people, exploited by landlords, employers, and merchants who put them in bondage to the time-payment plan. With bitterness, some eventually realize that they have landed at the bottom of the pecking order, in the spot occupied by the Negro back home.

Unlike other postwar immigrant groups—displaced persons from Europe, Japanese Americans from the West Coast, Southern Negroes—these people have not come here to build a permanent new life. A majority expect to stay just long enough to find work, save a little money, and leave when things get better "down home." Some do, and usually find that things are worse than ever, so they return North "for another spell." There is no desire to become a part of the community, and the community has no mechanism for helping these people who have cut themselves adrift.

The best estimate is that approximately thirty thousand Southern whites may be "a-stayin'" in Chicago at any given time. There is constant turnover as families move in and out of the shabby neighborhoods they share with Mexicans, Puerto Ricans, American Indians, and a few Negroes. . . . Battered automobiles bear license plates from Alabama, Georgia, West Virginia, Kentucky, and Tennessee. The auto often is abandoned after it brings the family to Chicago, but not before every saleable part has been stripped off. In one ninety-day period, more than four hundred abandoned cars were towed to the city auto pound from one square-mile section. Uptown's three-story brownstone and graystone apartment buildings have been carved into tenements where rents run $15 a week for a single room. An entire family often crowds into one or two rooms and several families will share a bathroom or kitchen, living by standards that may have been perfectly acceptable where they came from. Back home, garbage thrown into the yard was eaten by the animals; in the city it just accumulates.

And there's a difference in social mores that can get a man into trouble in the city. If you fight with your wife, for example, annoyed neighbors will call the police. At the end of the day down home, the workingman and his friend passed a jug around as they sat on the front porch to watch the sunset. There's no porch in Chicago, so they chip in for a six-pack of beer and settle down on the curb in front of a Wilson Avenue saloon. A squad car goes by and the policemen order the curbstone drinkers to move along. They protest that they aren't doing anything wrong, so the cops give them a routine frisking and come up with a couple of hunting knives. Every able-bodied man carried one down home, but it's against the law in the city and they're hauled off to jail for carrying concealed weapons.

Anyone who gets in trouble and has a rural accent is called a hillbilly, although less than half actually come from the hill country. The majority are miners or farmers from the red-earth flatlands. Chicagoans are convinced that these Southern whites have unleashed a crime wave on the city. Life in Uptown is not exactly peaceful, but police in the district say it's not any worse than other overcrowded neighborhoods. Most of the crimes committed by the Southerners are against each other—stomping on a man in a tavern brawl, wife beating, child neglect, a little more incest than in other groups, public drunkenness, and small burglaries that usually are bungled. Police Commander Captain John P. Fahey has pointed out that the Southerners are younger than other immigrants—mainly in their twenties or early thirties—and have a natural tendency to settle differences by direct action.

"We've had a job educating the community toward these people," he explained. "I'd say that drunkenness and fighting are their two biggest problems, but we only notice the ones who get into trouble. Most of them go about their business like everyone else. They come to the city and find we're not friendly. They're used to living in a rural area where people live far apart yet are close together. Here, they're living close together and people stay far apart. They had religion down there, but they don't have their churches up here, so they stop going to any church at all."

. . . Until now, the Southern whites have been ignored by Chicago's politicians because few stay long enough—or have the inclination—to become registered voters. . . . Republican Alderman Robert J. O'Rourke, has found his Southern constituents to be proud people, in many cases too proud to ask for help via the relief rolls. Even if they wanted it, many lack the residency requirements to be eligible for the various city, county, and state welfare programs.

O'Rourke considers it "a one-generation problem" that can be solved by reaching the children through the schools and boys' clubs. The schools in Uptown have been all but surrendered to the Southerners. Residents of the luxury apartment buildings on the nearby lakefront have taken their children out of the public schools and sent them to private institutions, claiming that the influx of a transient, backward population has lowered school standards. Elementary schools in the area experience a fifty per cent change in registration each semester. There is a high truancy rate and it is not unusual to find a thirteen-year-old with the reading ability of a second-grader. The schools have placed these older children into special remedial classes where they will be helped but not humiliated, and at the same time will not slow the progress of others. . . .

Another serious problem is what to do about the children when they're not in school. The Southern children don't stay long enough to organize into street gangs. Their kind of delinquency is petty theft to get some of the things other children have.

. . . One of the neighborhood's organized facilities is the Robert R. McCormick branch of the Chicago Boys Clubs. . . . Fred L. Lickerman, assistant executive director of the Boys Clubs, previously worked with other immigrant groups. He finds the Southerners and their children very different:

"The people we're dealing with are caught in an economic trap. They just don't understand what's in store for them up here. This is not their community and they don't want to get involved because they're not staying. The immigrants from Europe and other places had the formalized structure of the ghetto to take care of each other. It gave them a community of their own to fit into. These Southern people have a ghetto in a geographic sense, but it has no community organization and the children feel this insecurity.

"In the children we see a general deterioration of health—poor teeth, malnutrition, bad eyesight, hernias. There is a lack of education, but a great appreciation for the outdoors which you don't see in a city kid. We see politeness—'Yes, sir,' 'No, ma'am'—but a fear of not being accepted and a willingness to fight if they're laughed at for their clothes or the way they talk. There's a longing to be back home, because the city is frightening with its traffic, tall buildings, and un-friendly people.

"So we try to use our recreational facilities as a tool for guidance. To a child, play is his whole life. This is the place where a kid can meet a friend and find an adult who cares what happens to him. He can learn to cope with the street traffic, to become city-wise. We're trying to bring out the things these kids have to offer."

Nine-year-old Danny Ray is a member of the club and learned to cross streets the hard way. A year ago, when he first arrived in the city, his system was simple: "I just closed my eyes and hoped no car would hit me." Chasing a fire engine one day, he dashed into the street and was struck by a car. The boy suffered a fractured skull and the driver skipped bond, leaving Danny's family to pay the hospital bills. He lives with his father, mother, four brothers, and a sister in a four-room apartment on the first floor of a Kenmore Avenue roominghouse. The home, clean despite the crowded condi-tions, is decorated with religious pictures and old Christmas trinkets. The Rays come from Madison, West Virginia, where Danny's father, Harold, worked at a sawmill and cut brush for the state road department. He is thirty-four years old with a sixth-grade education. He sums up his plight by saying: "You can't buy a job these days if you don't know how to run a machine. I worked at just any job I could get, but there isn't much in West Virginia." In Chicago, he caught on doing maintenance work around a factory for $1.40 an hour, but for the past five months he hasn't been able to find steady employment. His wife earned the rent money by helping to manage the apartment building. . . .

Would they be better off back home? "Well, so far I think we're better off up here because things are even worse down there. I didn't like Chicago at first, but I'm satisfied now if we can just get work. When our friends go back they find nothing's changed."

The basic solution of the problem probably lies back in the home states where nothing has changed. . . .

William Meyers, a Chicago member of the Council of the Southern Mountains, Inc., is convinced that the problem eventually must be solved down South where it all began, but he emphasized:

"These people *are* coming here, now, and they face a spiritual and cultural isolation as well as a physical isolation. You have to admire them because they've had the guts to move from places where their families have lived for more than a hundred years. Their ancestors were the pioneers in this country, and they certainly have as much right as anyone to share in the American dream—whether it's 'down home' or in Chicago."

The Puerto Ricans in New York

NATHAN GLAZER

New York City had 500 persons of Puerto Rican birth in 1910; 7,000 in 1920; 45,000 in 1930. . . . During the war . . . there was almost no addition to the Puerto Rican population until 1944. Then there was a heavy migration of 11,000. The next year, with the end of the war, air service between San Juan and New York was introduced, which immediately transformed the situation of the potential migrant. In 1945, 13,500 entered the city; in 1946, almost 40,000: New York was in the middle of a mass migration rivaling the great population movements of the first two decades of the century. By 1961, there were 613,000 people of Puerto Rican birth or parentage in the city (representing about 60 per cent of the total number of Puerto Ricans in the continental United States). Since 1961, the number of new arrivals has fallen off sharply . . . however . . . a great many of the newcomers live in a veritable sea of misery.

As to its extent: Puerto Rican median family income was considerably lower than even non-white median family income—$3,811 as against $4,437—in 1960, and unemployment among Puerto Ricans also seems to be consistently higher than among non-whites. The census of 1950 showed, for men, 7 per cent of the non-Puerto Rican whites, 12 per cent of the Negroes, and 17 per cent of the Puerto Ricans unemployed; for women, 5 per cent of the non-Puerto Rican

§ Nathan Glazer, "The Puerto Ricans," reprinted from *Commentary*, vol. 36, no. 1, July 1963, pp. 1–9 (copyright © 1963 by the American Jewish Committee), by permission of publisher and author.

whites, 8.5 per cent of the Negroes, and 11 per cent of the Puerto Ricans. In 1960, 5 per cent of all New York males, 6.9 per cent of non-white males, and 9.9 per cent of all Puerto Rican males were unemployed.

In explaining misery among the Puerto Ricans, their high birth rate must be taken into account. Puerto Ricans begin bearing children younger, and bear more of them. A 1950 analysis showed that for women between the ages of fifteen and nineteen the Puerto Rican birth rate was about five times the continental white rate (the Negro rate for this age group was almost as high); for women twenty to twenty-four it was almost twice the white rate, and a third higher than the Negro rate.

We see the strain in a number of ways. For example, it is interesting to note how many of the adjusted Puerto Rican families have only one or two children. The job at $50 a week, which manages to support a small family in an apartment in the Bronx and which, compared with the $12-a-week income that was left behind on the island represents real advancement, is completely inadequate to support five children or more. All problems tend to pile up. The bigger family may not get into a good apartment or a housing project. The crowding in a small apartment may mean more illness and poor management of children. And the difficulty of feeding so many mouths on $50 a week means that welfare has to be called in to help. One-half of all families in New York receiving supplementary assistance from the Department of Welfare are Puerto Ricans; one quarter of all Puerto Rican children in the city are on some form of assistance; and about one-seventh of all Puerto Ricans are on public assistance. The Puerto Rican (especially the Puerto Rican male) is not happy about going on relief; no one is, but it is perhaps even worse for Puerto Ricans since their culture places so high a value on maintenance of dignity and self-respect.

Everything can contribute to breaking this circle of dependency—more education, more training, fewer children, fewer illnesses, better housing, dedicated social workers, etc., etc. Sometimes, however, at the bottom of the scale, things are too far gone for the circle to be broken. Here are the "multi-problem" families, afflicted simultaneously by a variety of miseries—a child who is a drug-addict, another who is delinquent, a father who is psychologically or physically unable to work, or perhaps is not there at all.

One of the greatest misfortunes of this bottom layer of unfortunates who cannot help themselves is the enormous difficulty of managing one of the most complex and ingrown bureaucracies in the world—harried city employees, probation officers, welfare workers, rent administrators, etc., etc., etc. An equal misfortune is the housing situation, which consigns those without sufficient resources and without energy to the frightful one-room furnished dwellings carved out of brownstones and apartment houses principally on the West Side of Manhattan. Better living quarters are available, and at cheaper rents, in the Bronx and Brooklyn, but when one is overwhelmed by so many troubles, the energy to take the subway to look for an unfurnished apartment, to get together the few sticks of furniture and the minimal kitchen equipment (the Welfare Department will pay), is often literally beyond the capacity of many families. And so they migrate dully from one of these awful dwellings to another, scarcely better, a few blocks away. Meanwhile, one generation on relief gives rise to another.

. . .

And yet despite all this, there was not an exceptionally high rate of delinquency among Puerto Rican children during the 1950s. Today, a good deal of Puerto Rican violence consists of crimes of passion involving members of the community only. . . . As for that other index of social strain—illness—Puerto Ricans seem to enjoy poorer health than other groups in the population, and their rate of admission to mental hospitals is higher than on the island, or for New Yorkers in general. The migration, it seems, has hit them very hard.

A typical pattern of migration for families with children is for the father to go alone, stay with relatives or friends, find a job and living quarters, and then gradually bring over the rest of the family. Many families are consequently divided between Puerto Rico and New York, and when they are united, if ever, they show wide differences in degree of knowledge of English, assimilation, and the like. A second pattern of migration involves a woman with children—her husband has deserted her, or she has decided to leave home and go to New York, where jobs are abundant, where the government is reputed to be "for the women and the children," and where relief is plentiful.

The Puerto Rican mother works here much more often than she does in Puerto Rico, but women still tend, if at all possible, to stay home to take care of the children. The boys are praised for their manliness and aside from being required to act respectfully toward their fathers (whether or not their fathers still live with their mothers), they are left to raise themselves. In radically different fashion, the girls are carefully watched, warned to keep their virginity—without which a proper marriage is inconceivable—and then relatively early they flee from this restrictive and stifling atmosphere into marriage and motherhood.

In New York, however, both traditional patterns raise serious problems. If the boys are left to themselves, they find bad friends, may take to drugs, will learn to be disrespectful and disobedient. And even if a boy survives the streets morally, how is he to survive them physically, with cars and trucks whizzing by, and tough Negro and Italian boys ready to beat him up at the slighest provocation? If the girls are guarded and confined to the home (i.e. a tiny, overcrowded apartment) as proper girls should be, they become resentful at a treatment that their classmates and friends are not subjected to.

Thus the radical boy-girl disjunction does not work in New York City. To the social workers or young ministers in the slums, the dances and other co-educational activities they run are means of teaching young boys and girls how to relate to each other in ways that are not purely sexual and exploitative, and perhaps in a measure they do accomplish this. But to the Puerto Rican (and often Negro) parents, what goes on in the settlement houses and the church socials simply looks like a shocking invitation to premature pregnancy.

In this confusing situation there are two possibilities. One is to give up altogether and simply let the children run wild. But a more typical reaction is a tightening of the screws, not only on the girls but on the boys, too. Many cases of disturbed Puerto Rican boys that come to the attention of social agencies are cases of overprotection, anxiety stemming from an exaggerated fear of the dangers of the streets. With the girls, a tightening of discipline makes life seem even more stifling, and there is less chance of escaping into an early marriage here than there is in Puerto Rico. When a social worker suggested to a Puerto Rican girl who had a job and was expected to scurry home from the factory as fast as she had from school, that she ought to get away from the traditionally strict supervision of her father by moving into a residence, the girl was shocked. "She seems to think that in Puerto Rico they would consider any girl who moves away from her family into a residence as someone who goes into a house of prostitution."

The changing city no longer provides the neighborhood that is exclusive to one ethnic group, and so the models for new conduct in rearing one's children vary. There are Negro, Jewish, and Italian models, as well as the "American" models of the welfare workers and the settlement houses. What degree of discipline is proper, what kind of punishment and rewards ought to be enforced, what expectations should one have of one's children? The Puerto Rican mother is at a loss in deciding on the right course.

And then there is the role of the school in the lives of the children. Even the least schooled migrant knows the value of education; Puerto Ricans universally would like to see their children well educated, and hope they will grow up to be professionals. But school is often a frustrating experience. The shift to a new language has been peculiarly difficult for the Puerto Ricans. We can only speculate as to why Jews and Italians, coming into the city at roughly the same ages as the Puerto Ricans have, and with less formal knowledge of

English to begin with, should have made a less problematic linguistic adjustment. Certainly the schools did much less to ease their path. (Of course in the years of the heaviest Jewish and Italian migration, the school-leaving age was considerably lower, so that the children who could not learn English got out before their problems became too noticeable.)

Probably no public school system has spent as much money and devoted as much effort to a group of minority children as the New York public school system has devoted to the Puerto Ricans. There are now hundreds of special personnel to deal with parents, to help teachers, to handle the special difficulties of students. The magnitude of the problem is barely communicated by figures. "On October 31, 1958," reports the Board of Education, "of the 558,741 children in our elementary schools, there were 56,296 children of Puerto Rican ancestry whose lack of ability to speak or understand English represented a considerable handicap to learning."

The numbers alone are enormous, and there is the additional problem of the rapid movement of the newcomers. On the West Side of Manhattan—one of the major sections of entry for Puerto Rican migrants—the turnover in an area containing sixteen schools has been 92 per cent, which means that each year the school confronts what is in effect a completely new student body.

It is probably particularly hard for adolescent boys to adjust to this situation, for the Puerto Rican emphasis on masculine dignity makes it embarrassing to speak English with an accent. Meanwhile, there is a good deal of school-leaving at the earliest possible age and relatively small proportions today go into the academic high schools. The register for New York City schools in October 1960 showed that 18 per cent of the elementary-school students, 17 per cent of the junior high-school students, and only 8 per cent of the high-school students were Puerto Rican. The proportion in the academic high schools was 5 per cent.

The other side of the coin is an impressive amount of activity by young, educated Puerto Ricans to raise the level of concern for education in the group. For example, Puerto

Rican social workers, professionals, and teachers have set up an organization called *Aspira,* which is devoted to helping students and their parents to take all possible advantage of educational opportunities. The young Puerto Rican leaders clearly see Puerto Ricans as following in the path of the earlier ethnic groups; and these leaders speak of the earlier ethnic groups as models for emulation, not as targets for attack. They identify, that is, with the Jews or Italians of forty years ago, rather than with the Negroes of today, and they have a rather hopeful outlook, which stresses the group's potential for achievement rather than the prejudice and discrimination it meets.

.   .   .

⟨ 16 ⟩

West 114th St.: A Place to Flee

GAY TALESE

More than five years ago, William, a quiet and disenchanted Negro boy who had been born in West Harlem, had been reared there and had just been mugged there, joined the United States Army not strictly out of patriotism—but also as a way of escaping West Harlem.

He was living with his parents on the fourth floor of a $40-a-month tenement. . . . His father was a dishwasher. His mother took in sewing. His neighborhood seemed without horizons; his block was known as a "hustler's street."

Yesterday, having been discharged from the Army, William

§ Gay Talese, "West 114th St.: A Place to Flee," reprinted from *The New York Times,* February 3, 1965 (© 1965 by The New York Times Company), by permission.

was back on West 114th Street. It is still called a hustler's street by those who dwell there, and he said it was "depressing to be home."

The announcement that $390,000 in antipoverty funds was being allocated to make 114th Street, between Seventh and Eighth Avenues, a model block was encouraging news to him, and others like him, but in a way it was too fantastic a promise—something they would accept better after it became a reality.

All along the street yesterday the talk was not about what would happen, but rather about what was happening on 114th Street. The proprietor of the P. & S. liquor store was telling how his place had been robbed three times in the last year; a teacher . . . was citing the abundance of problems . . . and William was trying to describe how being born on such a block leaves a mark that might not be easily removed by urban renewal.

"I have no ambition," he said. "Being born in this kind of neighborhood kind of pulls you down with it. I mean, nobody here likes to see you get any place."

Some boys with whom he grew up regarded the neighborhood school building across the street not as an institution of learning, but rather as a brick structure against which to bounce rubber balls. They also came to accept as commonplace the sight of elderly men, addicts standing and sleeping with their eyes open.

Rats running through the kitchen, electricity that did not work, door bells that never rang, frequent fires from electrical shortages, frequent robberies from drug addicts—all these things and more, as young William said, became a way of life on 114th Street when he was growing up, and still are.

· · ·

He had no heroes as a youth; nor did he have any desire to finish school. He and his close neighborhood friends were never arrested by the police, he continued, "but this is because we were lucky—we could run faster than the others."

In 1959 . . . he joined the Army. . . . After three years, he reenlisted. "I didn't want to come back to 114th Street."

But in the Army, he did not save a penny. He spent it all on furloughs—another symptom of his West Harlem heritage, he says.

After five years, eight months, and one day, he was discharged from the Army, largely because he felt he had, at the age of 25, to do something more with his life.

Yesterday, two weeks after leaving the Army, he was back in his parents' tenement.

. . .

On Feb. 15, he starts a part-time job at the "P.I. Diet" section of Bellevue; he does not know what "P.I. Diet" stands for, only that he will earn about $62 every 10 days on the job.

He still admits that he has "little ambition," but he hopes—and his friends hope—that 114th Street with antipoverty funds may change so he will no longer have to say of it:

"On 114th Street, there are no goals . . . nobody likes to see you get any place."†

(17)

Man With A Hoe, 1964

PAUL JACOBS

The park on the border of the Skid Row area in this California farm town is filled with men (and one or two women) sprawled out on the grass or sitting under the few trees.

---

† A complete renovation program is to be undertaken at 114th Street. In its 37, 5-story walk-ups live 1600 people in 380 families, 557 children under 18 years of age. The tenements with foundation—and federal—money will be renovated, there will be day-care centers, education classes, health clinics, etc. None of the original residents will be relocated.

§ Paul Jacobs, "Man With A Hoe, 1964," reprinted from *Commentary*, vol. 38, no. 1, July 1964, pp. 26–29 (copyright © 1964 by The American Jewish Congress), by permission of publisher and author.

Some of them are sleeping, their mouths open, their stubbled faces pressed into the ground; others are merely staring off into space. Here and there a bottle is being passed around a group, each man taking a deep swig before handing it on to the next. I count about a hundred of these near-derelicts from where I sit on a bench at the edge of the park. Later, as I walk by, they look at me incuriously. No one hails me as "Sir," and no one tries to make a touch. In my dirty pants, torn sweatshirt, and straw workhat, an old beachbag in my hand, I look like just another farm worker living on Skid Row.

On my way through the park to find a cheap hotel or flophouse for a few nights, the eyeglass case I have in my shirt pocket begins to feel uncomfortable, so I stop to take it out and put it into the bag. As I do I am struck by the fact that very few of these people in the park seem to wear glasses; in fact, I can spot only three who are either wearing glasses or have eyeglass cases in their pockets. And yet, nearly everyone in the park is in the age group that would normally need glasses.

Just on the outskirts of the Skid Row area, I find a hotel where I can get a room for $2.00 a night. Most day-haul farm workers would spend only a dollar, or at most $1.50, but I have learned how terribly depressed I get in the dirty, gray flophouses that are the only homes so many farm workers know. Skid Row not only houses bums, outcasts, and voluntary exiles from society, but blurs at the edges to take in the old and the poor as well. For where else can a badly paid worker find a place to sleep for $2.00 or less?

I pay the $2.00 in advance—all rent in such "hotels" is paid in advance, either by the day, the week, or the month—and take the key to the room in which I will be staying for the next few days before going on to spend a couple of weeks in a migrant workers' camp in the San Joaquin Valley. The room is about what I expect: peeling walls, a window with a tattered shade overlooking a dark airshaft, a broken bureau with a plastic doily on top, one wooden chair, a closet built into a corner, and overhead, a light bulb swinging on a chain.

There is no lamp by the bed—who reads in such a room at night?

My next stop is the farm labor office on the other side of the Skid Row area. Walking down a street past tong houses, Chinese shops and restaurants, Filipino barber shops and social clubs, and Mexican bars, I notice a small store with the word "Shoeshine" crudely lettered across the window, obviously, though, it isn't shines the three gaudily dressed Mexican women inside are selling. One of them catches my eye as I go by and shouts, "Hey, sport, come on in!"—waving her arm to show me the curtained recess at the back. Such girls service the Skid Row community, including fringe groups like the Filipinos. The most skilled of all the farm workers in Skid Row—they generally harvest asparagus, Brussels sprouts, and the early grape crop—many of these Filipinos have been in the area for more than twenty years without their families, and these women represent their only sexual contacts. Because they have no wives and the law once prohibited inter-marriage, the Filipinos reportedly suffer from a high rate of venereal disease. Yet they tend to be neater and cleaner than their neighbors on Skid Row, and when they dress up in their big-brimmed hats, wide-seated pants, and heavily padded jackets, they remind one of sporty gangsters in a 1930s movie.

It is early afternoon by now, and the farm labor office—whose hours are from 5:00 A.M. to 2:00 P.M.—is very quiet. Two men are sitting behind a counter (there are no chairs or benches on my side of the counter). I announce that I want to register for farm work, and wait while one of them checks to see if I have registered before at this office. Satisfied that my name isn't listed in any of his files, he motions me behind the counter to his partner's desk. "Can I see your social security card?" the man at the desk says. I take out my wallet, now thin and flabby without the thick bundle of credit cards I've left back home in San Francisco, and show him the social security card.

"Were you in the Army, Paul?" He uses my first name as a matter of course, even though I am at least ten years older than he is and he has never seen me before. I say that I was, giving him the little photostat of my Army discharge I carry with me on these trips. Then he asks me what kind of farm work I've done, and I tell enough of the right lies to get a green card from him with my new occupational title printed on it: "Farm hand, general."

"Is there much work?" I ask. "No," he answers, "the asparagus is about finished, but if you'll do stoop labor, you can work until the freeze in the fall. Be here tomorrow morning at 5:00 A.M. to get on the bus."

For the rest of the afternoon and evening, I walk around Skid Row, going from one dingy card room to another, where $2.00 will get you into a game of draw poker, lowball poker, or pan. The games are run by the house, which takes a chip from each pot in exchange for supplying the chairs and tables and a man to keep an eye on the betting. As for the players, they are a mixed group of Mexicans, Filipinos, whites, and Negroes; and there are even a few young fellows who look as though they go to college and just come down to Skid Row for the cards.

I eat my dinner in one of the many grimy restaurants in the neighborhood. The floor is littered with napkins, the counter is greasy, and sugar is spilled around the rack holding the condiments. A pleasant Mexican waitress serves me watery tomato rice soup, fatty lamb stew with potatoes and rice, diced beets, and one slice of canned pineapple. The meal costs eighty-five cents, and I buy a nickel cigar on my way out. Again I wander the streets, indistinguishable from the other men shifting a frayed toothpick around in their mouths.

It is nightfall now. Skid Row is crowded; the bars are jammed with beer and sweet-wine drinkers; the drunks stagger into the street and collapse in the alleys. For many of these men, Skid Row is the end point of some personal tragedy—perhaps a divorce, or alcoholism, or unexpected unemployment. Then the police cars make their appearance. They cruise slowly around the area, circling it like keepers in a zoo. One of them pulls up to the corner where I'm stand-

ing talking with three asparagus cutters, and the officer behind the wheel looks at me. "Hello, there," he says. As I
return the greeting, I notice him remarking to his partner,
"That's a new face around here." He will keep my face in
mind—just in case.

Back at the hotel three very old men and one middle-aged
farm worker are sitting in a row in the lobby, dozing intermittently through a re-run of an "I Love Lucy" show on TV.
I watch too for a while and then walk upstairs to my room.
It is hot and stuffy. Undressing, I wonder what the tempera-
ture in the room gets to be during the summer when the
valley becomes a furnace, made habitable for most of its
residents only by air-conditioners.

The work day begins at night. At 4:00 A.M., wakened by
the body noises of the man in the next room, I struggle out
of my narrow, lumpy bed. As I wash, I can hear him washing;
I brush my teeth, but he doesn't; and neither of us shaves.
Outside it's still dark. In my dirty work clothes, I eat breakfast—a "short stack with bacon"—at the counter of a nearby
all-night restaurant. After finishing the heavy pancakes
soaked in thick syrup and drinking two mugs of coffee, I buy
a box lunch from the Chinaman at the cash register to take
with me out to the fields. For fifty-five cents I get three
sandwiches of dry, thinly sliced roast beef with a piece of
lettuce on soggy white bread, an orange, and a small Danish
pastry.

Outside, crowds of men are heading toward the farm labor
office where the contractors' buses pull in to pick up their
loads of dayhaul workers. In the office, under a sign that says,
"Do not spit, sit, or lie on the floor," I line up with about
twenty-five other men, moving slowly toward the desk at which
work is being assigned. Everybody is wearing some kind of
hat or cap for protection against the hot sun, and the soiled,
ragged clothes which are the day laborer's uniform and
stigma. In my hand, I hold the green registration card that
will get me on the bus if there is work to be had. The only
jobs listed on the board today are cutting asparagus, and
short-handled hoe work on tomatoes or beets. Asparagus is

cut by crews and is a comparatively skilled job—much more desirable than such stoop labor as hoe work. But I've never done any asparagus cutting and so I have to take tomatoes or beets.

"Don't send anybody in who won't work short-handle hoe!" one of the three men behind the counter of the employment office shouts angrily after one of the workers has refused the job. Because short-handle hoe work is back-breaking and pays badly, there is often difficulty in finding enough men to fill the contractors' quotas.

"Beets or tomatoes, Paul?" asks the young man at the desk. I choose tomatoes, even though they pay only $1.00 an hour as against $1.10 for beets. But beets, I know, are much harder to work.

By 5:15 A.M. the big yard next door is jammed with men waiting to be assigned to a contractor's bus. Only one or two of the huge California farms do their hiring directly; most of the others deal with the labor contractors who set a flat price for supplying the workers to handle a particular job. The contractor then pays the workers out of this flat fee, naturally keeping enough for himself to make a profit. Some of the contractors are decent employers, but some are known as chiselers, to be avoided if at all possible. Even so, the difference between the best and the worst is only a matter of small degree; most farm workers are subjected to conditions long banished from modern industry.

More than half the men in the loading yard are Mexicans. Somehow, their Spanish sounds more educated than the English of the whites and Negroes greeting their friends and talking about how they made out yesterday. One slightly tipsy Negro is jumping around playing a guitar very badly; the more everyone ignores him, the harder he strives to get their attention. The asparagus crews are the first to be assigned to buses; they all have cheap plastic goggles on their hats which they will later use to keep the heavy dust out of their eyes. Finally, from the back end of the yard I see a contractor coming for my group. He is recognizable immediately by his baseball cap, his leather jacket, his boots and, most of all, his assured manner. He stops to kibitz a bit with the man from the employment office, and it becomes obvious that the relationship between them is much different from the one each of them has with us. Even though we farm workers are formally the clients of the state employment service, the real clients are the contractors, for they are permanent while we are only temporary; we are dependent upon both of them; and besides, they are social equals and we are their social inferiors. It is to the contractor, who needs it least, and not to the worker, who needs it most, that the state gives the benefit of its publicly supported employment service: the state is the instrument that provides the contractors with a good income and the growers with a pool of extremely cheap labor.

We board an old bus, painted blue, with the name of the contractor stenciled on the outside. In front of me, two Mexicans are chatting in Spanish, and across from them another Mexican sits alone. There are also eight other men in the bus—three Negroes and five whites, including myself. We sit and doze in the chill dark air, and then, at 6:00 A.M., when the buses in front of us start leaving the lot, our driver, who is Mexican, comes back with six more workers—three young white men, a Negro, and two Mexicans. Only one of the group, I notice, is wearing glasses. A few minutes later, we swing out of the lot and drive out on the highway.

By this time it is daylight and I can see the interior of the bus more clearly. On the dashboard is stenciled "Speed Limit 45 MPH," the maximum speed the state law allows farm buses to travel. I know these buses are supposed to be inspected by the state, but this one must have had its inspection a long time ago. The rear-view mirror is broken in half and the speedometer doesn't work at all. On the floor is a fire extinguisher, but it doesn't appear to be in very good working order either. Next to the driver is a large old-fashioned milk can filled with water. Once we get on the highway, the driver starts speeding, and we go barreling along until the contractor catches up to us in his pickup truck and signals the driver to stop. The driver gets out and I hear the contractor tell him in Spanish to slow down because the police are on the highway.

The driver gets back in the bus and begins going more slowly. But soon he is accelerating again, and in a few minutes we are moving at about the same speed as before. Some thirty-five minutes later, we turn off the highway and drive another three or four miles to a huge field with tomato plants growing in long straight furrows. Leaving our lunches on the seats, we file out of the bus, and the driver hands each of us a brand new hoe, about fifteen inches long with a head that is set back at an angle toward the handle.

In the field waiting for us is the contractor, talking with a stocky Nisei in his early forties. The Nisei tells us, in perfect English, to thin out the plants which are now about three inches high and growing close together. We are to chop out the row, leaving only one or two of the plants in each cluster, nipping off the weeds growing around them, and making sure that there is a space of from four to nine inches between the remaining plants. We station ourselves at every other furrow so that when we get to the end of the field, each of us can come back along the next row.

To chop at the tomato plants with a fifteen-inch hoe requires bending over almost double, and in only a few minutes, the sweat is pouring down my face. I soon fall behind almost all of the workers in the field: the end of the furrow seems a million miles away, and it takes me a half hour to get there. The bus driver, who is now acting as straw boss, keeps an impatient eye on me. He complains that I am not thinning the plants enough, and he tries to show me how to move my feet so that I can stay bent over. But the Nisei foreman tells me to take my time and do the job properly. As I get to the end of the row, the muscles in my back, thighs, and calves ache from the strain. Working my way back on the next furrow, I am acutely conscious of the straw boss watching and checking on me. By now, I am streaming sweat and in agony from the bending over. In the next furrow, an elderly man is working almost as slowly as I am, muttering to himself, "This here work's too hard, this here work's too hard."

"You ever done this kind of work before?" I ask him. "Sure," he answers, "I never done nothin' but farm work all my life, but this here's too hard. I'm too old to be bending over like this." Then, as I watch, he opens his pants and begins to urinate, never breaking the rhythm of his work, one hand hoeing, the other holding his organ with the urine dribbling through his fingers and down onto his pants.

And so the day moves on, with the sun rising in the sky and the heat rising in the field. The furrows extend into an eternity of tiny tomato plants and dirt, and the short-handled hoe is an instrument of torture. At last we take a break for lunch, after which a few of the men walk out into the field to defecate, scraps of newspaper stuck in their back pocket. Then hoeing again until shortly before four, when we quit and are driven a few miles to the labor camp, a small group of battered shacks in which crews are housed when they are working by the week. We line up at the contractor's office and are paid eight dollars for the day.

On the drive back to town the men talk more than they have all day, mostly about which bar serves the best beer for the money. In front of me, there is a discussion of how to beat the blood bank system. Selling blood is a good way to supplement your income. The only problem is that you can't give blood more than once every few months, and the date on which you sell the blood is marked on your fingers in ink that becomes visible under fluorescent light and won't wash off even with strong detergents. But one of the men has discovered that you can erase the ink by rubbing tobacco very, very hard over your fingers for a long time.

The bus stops on the street where the farm labor office is located, and we pile out. All around us, buses and trucks are pulling in to discharge their cargoes. Some of the men head for their rooms to wash off the dust and dirt; others make for a bar to get a beer or two first. Then there is the lamb-stew dinner again, and again the walk along the streets, the stopping on corners, the surveillance by the police, and maybe, if a couple of guys get together, the buying of a "jug" to knock off before bed. At 4:00 A.M., the work day will start again.

If you want to and have the strength to make it, you can go out to the fields six days a week and earn $48.00. Stoop labor is available in California for eight or nine months of the year, so you might, putting in six days a week, earn up to $1700–$600 more than the average wage of a farm worker in 1962. If you get sick, you earn nothing, and when the work season is over, you receive no unemployment insurance. Thus eventually you have to move on to another town, looking for another job which offers exactly the same conditions. And since you can never save enough to escape from Skid Row, it is easy to slip just a notch or two down to the bum level. At $1.00 an hour for back-breaking labor performed under the worst physical conditions, what possible incentive is there to work?

All this—when the government subsidizes crops and livestock, and when it has been estimated that doubling the wages of stoop labor might increase the retail price of tomatoes by a *penny* a can or a pound.

(18)

The Outskirts of Hope

MARY W. WRIGHT

. . . I know a man, I'll call him Buddy Banks. He lives in a ravine in a little one-room pole-and-cardboard house he built himself, with his wife, their six children, and baby

§ Mary W. Wright, "The Outskirts of Hope," reprinted from *Mountain Life and Work*, vol. 15, no. 1, Spring, 1964, pp. 10–15, by permission of the author and the Council of the Southern Mountains.

granddaughter. Mr. Banks, 45 years old, is a sober, kindly, passive man. He can read and write a little, has worked in the coal mines and on farms, but over the years he's been pretty badly battered up and today is "none too stout." Last fall, when he could no longer pay the rent where he was staying, his mother-in-law gave him a small piece of ground, and he hastened to put up this little shack in the woods before the snow came. If, as you ride by, you happened to glance down and see where he lives, and see his children playing among the stones, you would say, "White trash." You would say, "Welfare bums."

When the newspaper announced the new ADC program for unemployed fathers. I thought of Buddy Banks. There is not much farm work to be done in the wintertime, and Mr. Banks has been without a job since summer. Here in their ravine they can dig their coal from a hole in the hill, and dip their water from the creek, and each month he scratches together $2 for his food stamps by doing odd jobs for his neighbors, who are very nearly as poor as he is. Other than this there is nothing coming in. I thought, maybe here is some help for Buddy Banks.

Mr. Banks does not get a newspaper, nor does he have a radio, and so he had not heard about the new program. He said, yes, he would be interested. I offered to take him to town right then, but he said no, he would have to clean up first, he couldn't go to town looking like this. So I agreed to come back Friday.

On Friday he told me he'd heard today was the last day for signing up. We were lucky, eh? It wasn't true, but it's what he had heard and I wondered, suppose he'd been told last Tuesday was the last day for signing up, and I hadn't been there to say, well, let's go find out anyway.

Buddy Banks was all fixed up and looked nice as he stepped out of his cabin. His jacket was clean, and he had big rubber boots on and a cap on his head. I felt proud walking along with him, and he walked proud. (Later, in town, I noticed how the hair curled over his collar, and the gray look about him, and the stoop of his shoulders. If you saw him you'd have said, "Country boy, come to get his check.")

When we reached the Welfare Office it was full of people, a crowd of slouchy, shuffly men, standing around and looking vaguely in different directions. I followed Buddy Banks and his brother-in-law, who had asked to come with us, into the lobby, and they too stood in the middle of the floor. Just stood. It was not the momentary hesitation that comes before decision. It was the paralysis of strangeness, of lostness, of not knowing what to do. A girl was sitting at a table, and after a number of minutes of nothing, I quietly suggested they ask her. No, they told me, that was the food stamp girl. But there was no other. So finally, when I suggested, well, ask her anyway, they nodded their heads, moved over, and asked her. I wondered how long they might have gone on standing there, if I'd kept my mouth shut. I wondered how long the others all around us had been standing there. I had an idea that if I hadn't been right in the way, Buddy Banks just might have turned around and gone out the door when he saw the crowd, the lines, and that smartly-dressed food stamp girl bending over her desk.

Yes, he was told, and after waiting a few minutes, he was shown behind the rail to a chair beside a desk, and a man with a necktie and a big typewriter began to talk with him. They talked a long time, while the brother-in-law and I waited in the lobby. (They had asked the brother-in-law if he had brought the birth certificates. No, he hadn't, and so they said there wasn't anything they could do, to come back next Tuesday. He said nothing, stared at them a moment, then walked away. He stood around waiting for us all day long and never asked them another question. He said he would tend to it some other time. Fortunately, they got Mr. Banks sitting down before they inquired about the birth certificates.)

I knew what they were talking about: I have talked long times with Mr. Banks myself, and they were going over it it again, and again, and I could imagine Mr. Banks nodding his head to the question he didn't quite understand, because he wanted to make a good impression, and it would be a little while before the worker realized that he hadn't understood, and so they would go back and try again, and then Mr. Banks would explain as best he could, but he would leave something out, and then the worker wouldn't understand, so that, in all, their heads were bent together for almost an hour and a half. It seemed a long time to take to discover Buddy Bank's need—a visit to his home would have revealed it in a very few minutes, but of course twelve miles out and twelve miles back takes time too, and there are all those eligibility rules to be checked out, lest somebody slip them a lie and the editorials start hollering "Fraud! Fraud!" Actually, I was impressed that the worker would give him that much time. It *takes* time to be sympathetic, to listen, to hear—to understand a human condition.

At last he came out, and with an apologetic grin he said he must return on Tuesday, he must go home and get the birth certificates. Then they would let him apply. (How will you come back, Mr. Banks? Where will you get the $3 for taxi fare by next Tuesday? Perhaps you could scrape it up by Monday week, but suppose you come on Monday week and your worker isn't here? Then perhaps you won't come back at all. . . .)

While Mr. Banks was busy talking, I was chatting with one of the other workers. Because I am a social worker too, I can come and go through the little iron gate, and they smile at me and say, "Well, *hello* there!" We talked about all the work she has to do, and one of the things she told me was how, often, to save time, they send people down to the Health Department to get their own birth records. Then they can come back and apply the same day. I wondered why Mr. Bank's worker never suggested this. Maybe he never thought of it. (Maybe he doesn't live twelve miles out with no car, and the nearest bus eight miles from home. And no bus fare at that.) Or perhaps he *did* mention it, and Mr. Banks never heard him, because his head was already filled up with the words that went before: "I'm sorry, there's nothing we can do until you bring us the birth certificates," and he was trying to think in which box, under which bed, had the children been into them . . . ?

So I tried to suggest to him that we go now to the Health Department, but he didn't hear me either. He said, and he persisted, I'm going to the Court House, I'll be right back, will you wait for me? I tried to stop him: let's plan something, what we're going to do next, it's almost lunchtime and things will close up—until suddenly I realized that after the time and the tension of the morning, this was no doubt a call of nature that could not wait for reasonable planning, nor could a proud man come out and ask if there might not be a more accessible solution. And so, as he headed quickly away for the one sure place he knew, I stood mute and waited while he walked the three blocks there and the three blocks back. I wonder if that's something anybody ever thinks about when they're interviewing clients.

Mr. Banks and I had talked earlier about the Manpower Redevelopment Vocational Training Programs, and he had seemed interested. "I'd sure rather work and look after my family than mess with all this stuff, but what can I do? I have no education." I told him about the courses and he said, yes, I'd like that. And so we planned to look into this too, while we were in town. But by now Mr. Banks was ready to go home. "I hate all this standing around. I'd work two days rather than stand around like this." It wasn't really the standing around he minded. It was the circumstances of the standing around. It took some persuading to get him back into the building, only to be told—at 11:30—to come back at ten to one. (Suppose his ride, I thought, had been with somebody busier than I. Suppose they couldn't wait till ten to one and kept badgering him, "Come on, Buddy, hurry up, will you? We ain't got all day!")

I tried to suggest some lunch while we waited, but they didn't want lunch. "We had breakfast late; I'm not hungry, really." So instead, I took him around to the Health Department and the Circuit Court and the County Court, and we verified everything, although he needed some help to figure which years the children were born in.

At ten to one he was again outside the Welfare Office, and he drew me aside and said that he'd been thinking: maybe he should go home and talk this whole thing over a little more. He felt that before jumping into something, he should know better what it was all about. This startled me, for I wondered what that hour and a half had been for, if now, after everything, he felt he must return to his cronies up the creek to find out what it all meant. So we stood aside, and I interpreted the program as best I could, whom it was for and what it required, and what it would do for him and his family, while he stood, nodding his head and staring at the sidewalk. Finally, cautiously, almost grimly, he once again pushed his way into that crowded, smoke-filled lobby.

"Those who are to report at one o'clock, stand in this line. Others in that line." Mr. Banks stood in the one o'clock line. At 1:15 he reached the counter. I don't know what he asked, but I saw the man behind the desk point over toward the other side of the building, the Public Assistance side, where Mr. Banks had already spent all morning. Mr. Banks nodded his head and turned away as he was told to do. At that point I butted in. "Assistance for the unemployed is over there," the man said and pointed again. So I mentioned training. "He wants training? Why didn't he say so? He's in the wrong line." I don't know what Mr. Banks had said, but what *does* a person say when he's anxious, and tired and confused, and a crowd of others, equally anxious, are pushing from behind and the man at the counter says, "Yes?" I butted in and Mr. Banks went to stand in the right line, but I wondered what the man behind us did, who didn't have anybody to butt in for him.

While Mr. Banks was waiting, to save time, I took the birth cetificates to his worker on the other side. I walked right in, because I was a social worker and could do that, and he talked to me right away and said, "Yes, yes, this is good. This will save time. No, he won't have to come back on Tuesday. Yes, he can apply today. Just have him come back over here when he is through over there. Very good."

At 1:30 Buddy Banks reached the counter again, was given

a card and told to go sit on a chair until his name was called. I had business at 2:00 and returned at 3:00, and there he was, sitting on the same chair. But I learned as I sat beside him that things had been happening. He had talked with the training counsellor, returned to his welfare worker, and was sent back to the unemployment counsellor, after which he was to return once more to his welfare worker. I asked what he had learned about the training. "There's nothing right now, maybe later." Auto mechanics? Bench work? Need too much education. There may be something about washing cars, changing oil, things like that. Later on. Did you sign up for anything? No. Did they say they'd let you know? No. How will you know? I don't know.

At last his ADC (Unemployed) application was signed, his cards were registered, his name was in the file. Come back in two weeks and we'll see if you're eligible. (How will you get back, Buddy? I'll find a way.)

It was four o'clock. "Well, that's over." And he said, "I suppose a fellow's got to go through all that, but I'd sure rather be a-working than a-fooling around with all that mess." We went out to the car, and I took him home. "I sure do thank you, though," he said.

While I'd been waiting there in the lobby, I saw another man come up to the counter. He was small and middle-aged, with a wedding band on his finger, and his face was creased with lines of care. I saw him speak quietly to the man across the desk. I don't know what he said or what the problem was, but they talked a moment and the official told him, "Well, if you're disabled for work, then there's no use asking about training," and he put up his hands and turned away to the papers on his desk. The man waited there a moment, then slowly turned around and stood in the middle of the floor. He lifted his head to stare up at the wall, the blank wall, and his blue eyes were held wide open to keep the tears from coming. I couldn't help watching him, and when suddenly he looked at me, his eyes straight into mine, I couldn't help asking him —across the wide distance of the crowd that for just an instant vanished into the intimacy of human communion—I asked, "Trouble?" Almost as if he were reaching out his hands, he answered me and said, "I just got the news from Washington and come to sign up, and . . ." but then, embarrassed to be talking to a stranger, he mumbled something else I couldn't understand, turned his back to me, stood another long moment in the middle of the crowd, and then walked out the door.

Disabled or not disabled. Employed or not employed. In need or not in need. Yes or no. Black or white. Answer the question. Stand in line.

It is not the program's fault. You have to have questionnaires, and questionnaires require a yes or no. There is no space for a maybe, but . . .

Nor is it the people-who-work-there's fault, for who can see—or take time to see—the whole constellation of people and pressures, needs and perplexities, desires and dreads that walk into an office in the person of one shuffling, bedraggled man—especially when there are a hundred other bedraggled men waiting behind him? You ask the questions and await the answers. What else can you do?

Then perhaps it is the fault of the man himself, the man who asks—or doesn't quite know how to ask—for help. Indeed, he's called a lazy cheat if he does, and an unmotivated ignorant fool if he doesn't. It must be his own fault.

Or maybe it's nobody's fault. It's just the way things are. . . .

SECTION V

CONCOMITANTS OF THE CULTURE OF POVERTY: SCHOOLS, HOUSING, JUSTICE, HEALTH

I T *is trivial to emphasize the connection between poverty and education. But only in fairly recent times have we become seriously concerned about the content of the curricula and the pertinence of the methods in the schools which serve the children of poverty. Even more recent is the insight that the child from the culture of poverty starts school with considerable handicaps in speech ability, in listening ability, in perception in general, and it is therefore not surprising that in many schools in the slums third grade pupils are on an average already one year behind in reading ability. Experiments, too new to be evaluated yet, have been started in New York and some other large communities with day-care centers geared towards helping the very young pre-kindergarten child to overcome some of his environmental handicaps.*

Two articles which are less concerned with techniques than with a general overview of the problem of the school dropout are reprinted on pages 136. Professor Friedenberg's "Ideology of School Withdrawal," contrasts the utility of the high school for the middle class child with its disfunctionality for the child from the present day slums, the potential dropout. Dr. Kerckhoff discusses some special projects and a "new breed" of educator in a more optimistic vein (page 147).

HOUSING

Can the poor be housed adequately? Alvin L. Schorr, explores this question in a research report concerned with an appraisal of the effectiveness of housing policies on the elimination of poverty. Excerpts from his book Slums and Social Insecurity which covers a wide carefully documented range of housing efforts, urban renewal, and other experiments in the housing field are reprinted on page 151.

JUSTICE

Equal justice before the law is an American maxim. But do we have it? There are many facets in our culture which deny this equality to the poor and ignorant and violate their personal rights. Junius Allison, the Executive Director of the National Legal Aid and Defender Association, describes those situations in the jails, in the criminal and federal courts, and suggests some measures to alleviate the worst impediments to the achievement of a measure of justice for the poor. Excerpts from his article on "Poverty and the Administration of Justice in the Criminal Courts" are found on page 165.

HEALTH

Three articles, pertaining to various aspects of health and sickness of the poor are included here. The first, Poverty and Health, an original contribution by Robert L. Eichhorn and Edward J. Ludwig of the Sociology Department at Purdue University, deals with differences in the mortality and morbidity of the well-to-do and the poor, the medical care available to the poor and the meaning which sickness and health have for them (page 173).

"Psychiatrists and the Poor," by Robert Coles, a research

psychiatrist to the Harvard University Health Services and a consultant to the Southern Regional Council, describes the difficulties in reaching and treating the poor patient with present day methods applied by middle class psychiatrists (page 181). The brief excerpt from the Hollingshead and Redlich study illustrates graphically Coles' points about differential treatment dependent on the class association of the patient (page 189). In the third article, Frederick S. Jaffe, vice president of Planned Parenthood of America, explores the reasons why many low income families remain outside the area of effective birth control (page 191).

(19)

An Ideology of School Withdrawal

EDGAR Z. FRIEDENBERG

Compulsory school attendance in the United States has been justified from the beginning as essential to democratic policy.

. . . So far as I know, public support of education in this country has never been justified on the grounds that education was beneficial to the individual student, except to the extent that this pertained to equality of opportunity. It is logical to argue that the individuals who share the responsibilities of citizenship must learn what they have to do in order to discharge them. . . . Public education . . . can also claim, for that reason, to be good for the future citizens themselves.

. . . The school may, indeed, benefit the child; but it doesn't have to in order to earn the right to retain him. In talking about the youngsters who drop out, therefore, I am not going to start with the assumption that they ought to be retained. My hunch is that a large proportion of the dropouts may be doing what is best for themselves under the atrocious circumstances that exist. But I do want to analyze those circumstances, and see why the schools have so little to offer these youngsters.

. . .

§ Edgar Z. Friedenberg, "An Ideology of School Withdrawal," reprinted from *Commentary,* vol. 35, no. 6, June 1963, pp. 492–500 (copyright © 1963 by the American Jewish Congress), by permission of publisher and author.

For the types of students it is designed for, the public high school and junior high school curriculum's function . . . is liturgical. This is not as true of elementary school, because the basic skills really work. If you read as you are taught there, you will understand at least the words; if you write, your words will be understood; if you follow the rules of arithmetic, your calculations will check out and your books will balance, though you may never have the remotest conception of mathematics.

High school, however, is another matter. What would happen to the businessman, or just citizen, who attempted to apply what he was taught in high-school civics to the actual power structure of his community or his country? Who learns to love reading, or to find the kind of reading he can love among the classics and the bitty anthologies of the high-school English course? High-school history, by and large, is not even propaganda, because nobody is expected to believe it or to be moved by it; it is received as official myth. We tell youngsters that the Pilgrims came to New England searching for religious freedom not in order to give them an understanding of the actual root values of Colonial New England, but in order to provide them with the relevant cliché about the relation of church and state in America, and to let them know that a good middle-class American thinks of "my religious affiliation" or "the faith of my choice." This keeps the youngsters from getting hung up on religion, like an Italian peasant or rural Southerner. As for high-school science, it has, since Sputnik, increased its work load enormously and often tries to duplicate the content of college science courses. But essentially, it serves not as an introduction to science but to legitimate the American middle-class epistemology; science proves that Truth is an aggregate of general principles induced from empirical data that observers can agree on. The function of science is to protect people from odd-balls by setting up the rules so that subjective feeling is discounted. The scientific method, then, becomes a way of separating ends and means. When we want to win an election, or spy on the Soviet Union, or redevelop a slum, we go about it scientifically—i.e., by defining what we are trying to do as a technical problem. Naturally, we care about the feelings of the people affected; people's emotions are a very important factor. That's why we have psychologists on our team.

It is even truer than the progressives have always maintained that there is no valid distinction between the curriculum and the extra-curriculum. What counts is the total experience of the student, and what he learns in both the classroom and the playing field is a posture, a pattern of anxieties and a pattern of responses for dealing with it. There is seldom any pleasure in scholarship or ideas as such; the classroom and the playing field alike are places where you try to make it, and learn the techniques for making it that alienate you least from your peers. The over-all rules are the same in both: learn the ropes; don't get hung up; always be friendly, sincere, and creative. And win!

The important thing about this familiar picture is that it is a picture of a totally instrumental institution. Nothing about the institution is meant to be valuable, here and now, for its own sake. I don't mean that high school students don't have any fun. Of course they do; in the suburbs, at least, the high school is a "fun place." But this sort of fun is a part of the social pattern to be learned; being "fun" helps you to make it as well or better than anything, and it takes a great deal of social skill which American adolescents, notably, do learn.

We have never had much interest in what education means and feels like to the youngsters who are subjected to it; only in what it might help them to make of themselves. Even the Supreme Court, in its decision against segregation, could not rest on the moral obloquy and insult that segregation imposes on Negro children; that was not enough. It had to support its position further by pointing out that a major reason why separate schools could not be equal even if they were identical was that the Negro students couldn't make the same contacts there that white students could in their school, and that this was what people really go to school for.

So it is: the Court has done our motives no discredit, but merely reaffirmed our tradition. The public school gives poor boys a chance to develop their potentialities, both by formal education and by providing an opportunity to mingle with and learn from their social superordinates. The commonwealth is then the richer for the skills they later contribute, which would otherwise have been forever lost. This is exactly the opportunity our dropouts need, and which they ought presumably to welcome. So what has gone wrong?

What has gone wrong is pretty complicated; but basically I think one might locate it in the schools' perennial assumptions about the nature of what they have had to offer the children of the poor. These assumptions were probably never valid; but both the school and the poor once believed them. Now, only the school continues to assert them, though no longer with much conviction.

The schools assumed that in order to get ahead in America the student had to learn not only a body of skills, but also a set of social conventions, increasingly subtle and refined as he climbed up the ladder. In school he was taught techniques for handling things and manners for getting along with people. The teachers were the transmitters of an alien culture —alien to them, too. Social mobility was a process like preparing to get a job as a rice farmer in China or a coffeegrower in Brazil. There was a strange language to be learned —from instructors who didn't speak it too well themselves; a strange body of techniques to be mastered—from teachers who had never practiced them at first hand. It would all have to be learned over again when he got there; but at the time it seemed relevant, and made the student feel that he was well on his way.

Now, there are three important ways in which this situation differs from the condition in the high school today. In the first place, the problem of dropouts did not then exist. Most of the students who drop out today would never have been in high school fifty years ago; the school-leaving age has risen irregularly over the past decades, and a more rigid and self-confident school policy would not have hesitated to keep students in grade school until they reached it, whatever it was, if they did not pass.

A good many of these dropped out, and took unskilled jobs, which existed. . . . They weren't a dropout problem; they were the working class.

But those who didn't drop out, even though they came from a working-class background, did not feel at the time that they were losing their identity. . . . In school you were still you: *striving* didn't separate you from other poor, immigrant boys; it was exactly what poor, immigrant boys were supposed to do. There was no intimation at the time that you were leaving yourself behind. It wasn't that you were becoming a different person; the old *you* was learning new tricks. Education was instrumental, all right—it has always been that in America—but the instruments were thought to be in the curriculum. The student didn't have to learn to think of *himself* as one.

And finally, nobody doubted what the norms were. It seemed very clear that the people in the next stratum up were the ones who knew what the student had to learn; he had to be able to do what they did. This wouldn't make them accept him willingly; but it would allow him to work his way in even if they didn't.

I don't mean to imply that the school actually delivered the social mobility it promised; sometimes it did, more often it didn't. But this was the way it was supposed to work, and why there was so little controversy over whether compulsory school attendance was good for the individual as well as for the commonwealth. As long as the students who stayed in school believed in education naïvely, it served—much better than religion could have in this heterogeneous country—as the opiate of the people. And opium vendors don't have dropout problems.

Apparently, however—to judge by the present situation—they can: the American poor are getting over their addiction.†

† Thus, in her recent study of the schools in Big City, Patricia Sexton reports dropout rates even in *elementary school* of 15.5 per 10,000 children from families earning from $3,000–$5,000 annually, falling to 3 children per 10,000 for families earning $5,000–$7,000. For families making more than $9,000, the rate was less than 1 child per 10,000. In high schools, of course, the rate is enormously greater, but follows the same

It takes more and more education every year to invoke the same dream; and reality breaks through too often, leaving them sick, mean, and edgy. The educational establishment, fearful of losing popular support, is naturally much concerned with the possibilities of a *rapprochement,* of which two have already been tried. The simplest of these is an effort to beef up the traditional, but paradoxically faltering, economic appeal of education. Students are reminded over and over that today, more than ever, you need a high school diploma to get any sort of job and a college degree to get a good one. They are given the statistics on the fabulous return education, as an investment, brings in over a lifetime in increments of annual income. The unemployment data on adolescents and unskilled labor are stressed so that the youngsters will understand how hopeless things will be for them if they drop out of school. If they and their teacher are sophisticated enough, the demographic shift in job-type may be explained: how unskilled and blue-collar work has fallen off, while service and white-collar jobs, demanding a higher level of school achievement, have enormously increased in proportion.

All this is true enough; but the implication is false. It does not follow that most of the students now dropping out would have a better chance, even economically, if they stayed in school. . . . In our economy, the demonstrable economic value of an education is partly a consequence of its scarcity. The blue-collar-white-collar figures are relative, and one loses sight of how much smaller the white-collar one was to begin with. The absolute increase in white-collar opportunity does not compensate for the absolute loss in blue-collar jobs—a discrepancy which is rapidly increasing in magnitude as automation proceeds. Today's dropouts are, perhaps fortu-

pattern. There is no high school in Big City whose median family income is less than $5,000. For schools with median family incomes ranging from $5,000–$5,999, Sexton found a dropout rate of 19.2 percent of the total registration, falling to 7.9 percent for schools whose students had a median family income of $7,000–$7,999, and to 3.6 percent for the school whose students came from families having median incomes above $9,000. (*Education and Income,* Viking, New York, 1961, pp. 97–202.)

nately, pretty skeptical kids; if they all believed that the
school could deliver them to a brighter economic future we
would soon have unemployed IBM operators and technicians
hanging around the way India and Africa have lawyers.

The other, and more sophisticated, *rapprochement* is represented by the Higher Horizons Program, about which I wish
I could bring myself to be less doubtful, for it is a program
that seems to me characterized by much intelligence, in-
genuity, enthusiasm, and sheer good will. Its appeal, moreover, is not purely economic. I understand it to be an attempt
to convey to students that middle-class culture, *in toto,* is
not beyond their grasp. It can be theirs, if only they do their
work. As the title implies, the Higher Horizons approach
seeks to make education appear more worthwhile to the
student, and encourages him to remain in school to develop
his potentialities, by raising his level of aspiration not just
economically but culturally. As the boy lifts himself to gaze
beyond the slum there comes into view the Museum of
Modern Art.

It is heartening to find the middle class so generously
willing to share its resources, and, for once, apparently con-
fident of their value. It is also obvious that if the middle class
cannot somehow make public education acceptable to the
poor on its terms rather than theirs, middle-class dominance
of public education—a long established fact of American
life—is doomed. . . .

The dropouts, by and large, don't like middle-class culture
and they know quite well what we can do with it. Dropping
out is one way of telling us, and it is about time we turned
our attention to the things about the school that are bugging
them. The school is the arena in which these youngsters en-
counter middle-class life; this is where the dropouts fight the
ten-year's ideological war that ends in their defeat and rout.
In this warfare the core values of their culture and the values
the school represents are at issue, and any one that we start
by considering will lead to the others. I think the most fruitful
might be the familiar question of deferred gratification, or

impulse control, which is the source of so much conflict with the school authorities.

We all know the school's side of the question; and know that lower-class youngsters act out their conflicts. Retention programs try to face up to this by helping the youngsters learn more self-control and giving them some valid experience of being rewarded for it, so that they will discover for themselves that certain very desirable goals exist that can only be achieved by people who plan, save, and give a soft answer to wrath-provoking circumstances. In this way the kids learn that there may be more desirable rewards than the immediate pleasure of blowing up and shooting your bolt.

. . .

. . . I think the youngsters who drop out are probably, in many ways, a more promising moral resource than those who stay in, and I think they are driven out in part by moral revulsion from the middle-class life of the school. They could never, themselves, identify their feelings as moral repugnance because they view morality as being on the side of the enemy and therefore square; they imagine they dislike morality and have never been allowed to realize that they have morals of their own. They don't have a complete moral *system,* because they are not systematic; they are unprincipled in their behavior, because principles are too abstract for them to handle. But in a concrete situation they can be trusted more safely than their middle-class peers who are trying to make it.

. . .

. . . They are ill-disciplined. They have no basic skills. They are so sore that any place you touch them hurts, and when they are hurt they hurt back. They are extremely parochial, limited in their experience of the world to a few city blocks of desolate slum, and therefore both gullible and suspicious about anything beyond it. They are sometimes homeless, and never have any quiet place to study and think. They are inconveniently aware of their own sexuality and inconveniently skilled at bringing it to the attention of others. They live, their teachers sometimes say, like animals. . . .

But if these youngsters are trapped, it is not in their apprehensions of pseudo-events. They are not alienated from themselves. They still have access to their sense-data, and, on their own terms, they are accustomed to fidelity.

Those are the qualities that, I believe, we hoped to preserve and continually renew by building an open society in which a sensitive, compulsively masculine boy could become an Ernest Hemingway and a poor but beautiful waif a Marilyn Monroe. But at this juncture, less fatal alternatives to mediocrity are needed. Can a school geared to success and social mobility help formulate them? Its traditions are against it, its staff is against it, its relationship to the community power structure is against it.

To reach the dropouts and give them a reason for staying, the school would have to start by accepting their *raison d'être*. It would have to take lower-class life seriously as a condition and a pattern of experience—not just as a contemptible and humiliating set of circumstances that every decent boy or girl is anxious to escape from. It would have to accept their language, and their dress, and their values as a point of departure for disciplined exploration, to be understood, not as a trick for luring them into the middle class, but as a way of helping them to explore the meaning of their own lives. This is the way to encourage and nurture potentialities from *whatever* social class. Talent, and genius, when real, are expressions of individual experience and the inner life. But success and higher status are not the first goal to which talent or genius is devoted—though they are sometimes the last.

I do not mean to imply that I accept Sitwell's Fallacy: that the poor are happier in their station in life and should be left to enjoy it. Most lower-class people of whatever age hate lower-class life, I am sure: the noise, and the filth, and the crowding, and the vulnerability to the police and illness; never feeling quite well or quite rested. Worst of all, perhaps, is the constant din of the mass media—including the school—telling them that if they were any good at all they would be middle-class people like everybody else, and live in loveliness in Larchmont. But the fact that they have reason to hate their life of fear and deprivation does not give us the right to force ours on them as the only acceptable alternative to it. This is something they must work out for themselves, and the school's job is to help them understand most fully the meaning and nature of what they have to work with. Basically, the problem of reaching the dropout is analogous to that faced by the Peace Corps in reaching the peoples of underdeveloped countries. Can we—do we even really wish to—help them deal with their situation on their terms with our resources, while leaving our way of life aside till somebody asks for it?

Frankly, I doubt it. This is not how the teachers I know approach lower-status youngsters. They are afraid of them, for one thing. The principal is afraid of disorder which looks bad in his record and in the records of his teachers, and they each have their careers to think of, too. So they learn early to keep the kids in line; this comes first. Order *is* helpful to learning, but it doesn't come first, it grows out of the common task; and teachers who put it first are not enthusiastic allies in keeping disorderly youngsters in school till a basis for order can be created. Order is not, to be sure, the central issue, but it will serve to symbolize the sharpness of the issue between those whose security depends on the suppression of impulse, and those who depend on its expression.

In the urban public school today, the former predominate, and I don't think they can be easily changed, within the limits of personality and bureaucracy that characterize the school. If they can be, there is no fundamental reason why the kinds of youngsters who now drop out may not be well served. But this is a big *if*, for the public school, as it is, is profoundly expressive of our culture. And the fate of the "dropouts" is just one more expression of their actual status in our democracy. . . .

❨ 20 ❩

The Problem of the City School

RICHARD K. KERCKHOFF

. . . The city school . . . has problems because the city
has problems—one aspect of which is the fact of racially and
economically segregated life. . . . For various reasons, many
Americans will no longer accept certain inequalities, discriminations, and inadequacies which used to be ignored or
seen as merely a normal part of life. In education, as in economics and in race relations, this situation provides an
American dilemma. When enough people decide not to put
up with a long-standing condition, yesterday's school condition becomes today's school problem.

No more than a few decades ago, there were undoubtedly
many locales in which the educational expenditure per child
was twice as high in the "nice" neighborhood as it was in
the city slum. People used to say, "That is the way things are."
But today more people are saying, "That is not how things
should be," and some cities now spend more for a child from
the "gray areas" than for a child from the advantaged areas.

There are more of these children of disadvantage today
than before. A current prediction is that they will make up
half the population of big-city schools by 1970. More and
more, then, the big-city school becomes the school of the
poor, and a major problem of the city school becomes the
problem of being poor.

Working with poor people is already the central problem

§ Richard K. Kerckhoff, "The Problem of the City School," reprinted
from the *Journal of Marriage and the Family,* vol. 26, no. 4, November
1964, pp. 435–439, by permission of author and publisher.

of the city school from the viewpoint of many educators. In a recent survey, teachers who were interviewed described their schools and their pupils primarily in terms of the difficulties poverty and cultural disadvantage brought about. More often than not, the teachers claimed that their jobs were made less satisfying and more difficult because the children:

Score low on IQ and other tests.
Read and speak poorly and perform below grade level on other tasks.
Are not motivated toward the academic goals teachers hold, such as completing high school, going to college, etc.
Are not well disciplined or taught good manners in their homes.
Are not clean.
Are not interested in school or in the future.
Cannot or will not learn.
Tend toward toughness, violence, listlessness, dishonesty, a perverted sense of humor, and sexual license.
Etc., etc.

The educators repeatedly charged that the parents of these children:

Do not encourage high academic performance, and even work against it.
Scorn teachers.
Do not attend school organization meetings such as the PTA.
Cannot provide school-community leadership when given tasks to perform.
Are cruel to their children and ignorant of child development.
Are difficult to deal with, unreasonable, and sometimes drunk and violent.

. . . Most of the teachers had very litle training, either pre- or in-service, for working with children in the gray areas. In fact, this kind of training is hard to find, which is rather strange when it is considered that teachers are provided with many other kinds of special education. Also, as compared with only a few decades ago, very few new teachers want to teach in the big city. Formerly, the graduate of a teacher's college was apt to make the big-city school system his first choice for a job; that is where the salary was good and the working conditions more ideal. Today, however, the new graduate probably prefers an appointment in the suburbs, and for the same old reasons.

The result of this kind of teacher personnel situation is quite often a serious problem of recruitment and morale. The teacher's concept of himself as a successful professional person is often damaged by the traumatic events of the first teaching assignment. Resignations and requests for transfers often follow this shock. Also, teachers grow psychological defenses against failure, such as rigid, self-protective philosophies which project the blame onto the children, onto their race, etc.

Much of the shock teachers often experience on their first big-city job can be analyzed in social class terms, and there has been great emphasis recently on the class differences which often pertain between teacher and pupil. To the extent that social classes are subcultures . . . people in different classes perceive, judge, value, interpret, and understand things quite differently. Their language is different, to a degree, as is their logic, motivation, and morality.

Failure either to recognize or to deal effectively with this cultural difference can lead to discouraging results. . . .

THE COUNTERATTACK

The first battle in the counterattack that big-city education has been making against the conditions described above came about with the recognition that the world of the school as reflected in textbooks, in the speech patterns of teachers, and in the whole motivational system of the school culture, is different from, and in many cases alienated from, the world of the culturally disadvantaged child. This recognition has led to some major attempts at improvement.

Attempted improvements have included making changes in the culture of the school, such as producing textbooks which contain pictures of other than middle-class white children. Changes in the culture of the child are most often attempted, such as enrichment through Higher Horizon-type field trips. Sometimes the attempt is to change the parent, as in the use of community social workers by some Great Cities projects, or to change the teachers, one of the efforts of the Banneker Group in St. Louis. Projects have also tried to improve matters by increased use of the school's physical plant for summer schools, twilight schools, Saturday schools, and community schools, so as to enrich the lives of deprived children and involve their parents in the educational process. Other approaches involve the use of nonprofessional or paraprofessional teacher aides, teaching machines, and TV.

In a Washington, D.C. School Project on Consultation Skills, the author and his colleagues have tried to take a somewhat less direct approach. Abundant evidence indicates the crucial role of the school principal in influencing the mental health and human relations climates for the children and adults associated with his school. The project attempts to better the learning climate in the city school by improving the principals' interpersonal relations skills and by marshaling the forces of mental health in their schools. Every principal is offered a three-part program in this four-year project. In Part I, workshops of 40 principals each focus on questions of communication and interpersonal relations in the school setting; in Part II, groups of 10 principals and two school psychologists work on mental health and relationship problems of their own choosing; and in Part III, each principal takes on an in-school project of his own with guidance from the School Project on Consultation Skills staff. These Part III projects have included in-service training of faculties to increase effectiveness in their particular neighborhood communities, and the study of human relations problems involving race and cultural deprivation. . . .

Perhaps more important than any of these big-city projects and plans, however, is something else that is happening in education. The largest and most impressive counterattack on big-city school problems is being made across the nation by the appearance of a new breed of professional person. This kind of professional is represented in other fields by the curbstone clergyman who works with his parishioners where they are instead of waiting for them to come into his church, and by the gang social worker who follows a similar approach with his street-corner clients. In education, the teacher and principal are beginning to appear who are not only successful with the hard-to-teach children, but who welcome placement in gray area schools because of the greater satisfactions they experience there. From interviews with teachers and administrators in several large cities, the author has hypothesized that the following principles apply to the educator who succeeds in the problem school where others have failed:

He has what is now being called an anthropological approach. He knows and respects other ways of life, but he does not have to abandon his way. He has a strong and healthy philosophy about human difference which includes a realistic view of human potential and human limitation.

He knows about lower-class people and the lives they lead. He cares. He knows how they view the professional person and that they often resist the professional person's most professional approach, speech, and dress. He has accepted and can work with resistances to his color, sex, and age where they exist.

He knows that people may not come to him—he may have to reach out to make contact with the student or with the parents. He believes that people cannot be expected to accept leadership until their respect has been *earned*. He knows that it takes time to be accepted and to establish rapport.

He is truly community-minded. His approach is much like that of the community development specialist in so-called underdeveloped countries. He understands community organization, hidden leadership patterns, etc. He has learned what worries the people in his neighborhood and what motivates them.

He knows and is enthusiastic about the content he is teaching.

In brief, along with being a good teacher, he has dealt successfully, and usually without ever conceptualizing the problem in social class terms, with the twin challenges of

(1) identifying with a subculture different from his own, and
(2) relating the somewhat alien institution, the school, to
the neighborhood subsociety. . . .

⟦ 21 ⟧

Housing Policies and Poverty

ALVIN L. SCHORR

Space, Structure and Poverty

. . . The poor person may visualize city space in a distinctive manner. He is, so to speak, a block dweller. He does
not feel at home outside his neighborhood, perhaps not any-
where farther than 10 or 20 blocks from his home. He is
no more a citizen of the city than was the kitchen maid of
former generations a citizen of her mistress' house. On the
other hand, the man who has more money is, in his own
mind, a city dweller. He conceives of the city as a totality,
from time to time he sees its parts, and he calls upon its
resources. In general, the amount of income he has distinguishes the city dweller from the block dweller, but not
always. The operative distinction is between those who com-
mand automobile and other forms of transportation and those
who do not. Consequently, a middle-class aged person may be
a block dweller, shaped by his past. A poor teenager may be
a city dweller, shaped by his future.

§ Adapted from Alvin L. Schorr, "An Appraisal of the Effectiveness of
Housing Policies in Helping to Eliminate Poverty in the United States,"
Slums and Social Insecurity, U.S. Department of Health, Education, and
Welfare, Social Security Administration, Division of Research and Sta-
tistics, Washington, D.C., Research Report No. 1, pp. 41–47, 64–73,
95–137.

As always, it is easier to describe a problem than to find a solution. Only city dwellers will avoid poverty in the future. The block dweller will have some difficulty in finding a job, let alone mastering the complex resources that determine how well he can be trained and serve his health and other needs. But one does not convert a block dweller by moving him. His orientation is a product of his background; moving him simply sweeps away the security he knows. We seek housing then that provides security for the block dweller, and a transition to city dwelling for those who can use it— perhaps especially a transition for their children.

How do we get such housing? It is, perhaps, clear that care must be taken to distinguish the areas of a city that require clearance from those that require rehabilitation. It has been pointed out that low rent areas have been confused with slum areas, and neighborhoods wiped out that might readily have been rehabilitated. Such neighborhoods, if they can be saved, are likely to be more suitable to the needs of poor families. The need to save them has gained adherents, if only because blight moves faster than rebuilding alone can. Recent legislation provides new financial aids for rehabilitation, but there will have to be care that the process of upgrading does not price housing beyond the reach of the people who are in it. Another solution is to offer slum dwellers rehabilitated houses, which may be in neighborhoods that are more acceptable, rather than congregate public housing.

.   .   .

. . . For poor people there are other important effects of the increasing separation of their living places from those of other people. Special problems are created in providing the more formal services (education, settlement houses) that are indicated. A very high quality of service is required in precisely the locations that funds are sparse and skilled professionals reluctant to work. Perhaps even more important, there develops the conviction among poor families that they are deliberately, if arbitrarily, sealed off from others. This is particularly the case, of course, for Negro families in neighborhoods segregated by color. . . . The issue, then, is not that they do not have neighbors from whom to assimilate values and techniques that will move them upward, but that their situation appears to prove how useless it is to try.

. . .

Poverty in the Midst of Change

. . . The problems of relocating families suitably are related to housing supply and the location of suitable quarters; to state of education and deep-rooted attitudes about family and . . . neighborhood; to a resentment of outside interference that might, in other circumstances, be admired; and to all the difficulties that lack of money produce. . . . Special kinds of services will need to be provided. At their best, these services include material aids: payment of moving costs, finder's fees for the location of suitable dwellings, and even redecoration of premises to induce owners to rent to displaced families. These services must include effective arrangements for the location of vacant houses or apartments and for early, professional appraisal of their suitability. Finally, of course, these services must provide for patient, realistic, continuous conversations between the displaced family and some helping person. The distinguishing characteristic of successful service programs is that they accept *primary* responsibility for families in designated renewal areas. Though it can hardly be said that the general picture of relocation has provided reason for applause, in some places excellent progress has been made. In a site undergoing clearance in New York City, for example, a special project successfully relocated two-thirds of a group that had been designated "hard core" and "undesirable."

How do relocated families make out in general? Upon examination, this fairly simple question turns out to be difficult to answer. The Urban Renewal Administration reports that, of 97,000 families relocated by the end of 1961, 92 percent had been rehoused in "locally certified standard housing." Eight percent had gone to substandard housing. (The circumstances of 16,000 families were not known and presumably would show a high percentage in substandard housing.) However, these figures represent 292 cities' separate definitions of standard housing and separate judgments about how firmly to hold to housing standards. A degree of skepticism about local reporting is in order, as localities will have declared that they are able to relocate families adequately in their applications for urban renewal funds. . . . Furthermore, only public housing and urban renewal have even in principal required the provision of suitable relocation; the record of highway and other public programs is, without doubt, worse.

For these, and perhaps for other reasons, city-by-city studies arrive at quite high proportions of relocated families in substandard housing. In 1957, Philadelphia found 70 percent of families dislocated by all programs living in quarters that did not meet the standards of the housing code. In Cincinnati, about half of those displaced find other housing of poor quality. Baltimore is a city that should have at least an average relocation record: it has had a comparatively high rate of housing vacancies and has invested a good deal of effort in relocations. A study of families relocated from a small urban renewal project in 1959 and 1960 concludes that 10 percent wound up in dilapidated housing and about 20 percent in crowded housing. In addition, families lacked central heating, electricity, hot water, or other essential facilities.

Between 1955 and 1958, the School of Public Administration of the University of Southern California gathered data from 41 cities about relocation for urban renewal and public housing. In 26 cities that provided little or no assistance with relocation, about 25,000 families were displaced. About 70 percent entered substandard housing in the same neighborhood. Some who remained in the neighborhood and most who moved elsewhere found adequate housing. The other 15 cities provided special assistance in relocation; they had about 17,000 families that were moved. About a third lived, in the end, in substandard housing. The magnitude of such findings as these leaves little room for comfort. . . .

Of the million families who will be displaced by urban

renewal in the next 10 years, half will be Negro. Many will have other disadvantages. . . . A large percentage will be poor. . . .

It is not only relocation that requires attention in the course of clearing and redeveloping land. The first hint that land is to be cleared catches up poor families in a dynamism that they did not seek and can only in minimal ways control. Neighborhood rehabilitation with spot clearance may have similar effect. . . . Relocation is the terminal point in the process of change; what comes before is easily as significant.

The process of change can be hopeful and it can be frightening. . . . The effect depends on the type of family and neighborhood that is involved. The effect depends also on the social and physical processes that take place. The questions that are imminent in change are readily brought to mind. Who has the right arbitrarily to move me or to force me to fix my house? Why me? Wouldn't I already have hot water if I could afford it? Will I get enough for my place to get a new one? Will we get along with the people who live there? Will they like us? When must we move? Can I prevent it? Will they get angry if I try to prevent it? Must we move to a project? Maybe it would be better. What will our friends think of us? Will they say our family is too large? Maybe I can have a decent kitchen. Will they say we're not good enough? How can we afford it? And last, as first: Why us? Not us!

.   .   .

An appearance of drift and uncertainty may be inevitable in areas facing clearance; these attitudes are readily transmitted to the residents. "Those who were not the first to go," writes a settlement house worker, "were further depressed by living in crumbling and deserted neighborhoods." The problem may be exacerbated where, out of a wish to provide housing somehow, families are moved from one group of houses to another as phases of demolition and building proceed. They live, almost of necessity, in houses that are poorly maintained and surrounded by litter and evidences of vandalism. Families find themselves poised for flight over a period of years. They may move within a narrow compass and be caught again and again. They also move, of course, simply because they do not achieve adequate shelter. The observation of multiple moves has been made in points as widely separated as Manhattan and Westchester County, N.Y., not to speak of San Francisco. The *Washington Post* describes a local situation as follows:

The 50-year-old father of 13 children started running in 1954, when he and his family were pushed out of an alley shack to "make way for white folks" coming into the Georgetown section. Since then, the family has moved seven times; always one step ahead of a rent collector or a housing inspector. Along the way, five older children have gone to other quarters. One child is in the Ashland, Ky., Federal Reformatory. The family is now one step ahead of a bulldozer. It lives in a row house slated for demolition.

· · ·

The impact of what we might call disorganizing change on almost any kind of family is self-evident. Energy and money are spent wastefully. Opportunities are missed. Mood is affected. A sense of loss persists beyond the time when new satisfactions might have been found. It may be worth underlining the precision with which disorganizing change reinforces those patterns of poor people that keep them poor. Apathy, orientation to the present, and a sense of helplessness are the attitudes that poor people's experiences have tended to produce. Such attitudes can only be confirmed by being caught up in a change that is not understood and does not *seem* constructive.

The importance of distinguishing disorganizing change from constructive change may be clarified by comparing poor, mobile families with construction workers who live in trailers. Few types of American families are as mobile as construction workers. Yet they have cohesive families and lives that are normally satisfying. Many achieve a high standard of living. When one inquires why they do not find frequent moves disturbing, it appears that they have learned to "settle in" each community. Though they may live a year or less in a particular trailer court, they are apt to build a porch and plant trees. They live as if geographically stable. In contrast, the poor families of whom we speak live as if waiting for a blow to fall, unable to risk energy that will not be repaid on the spot, and reasonably certain that they are not their own masters. There is, no doubt, a degree of change so great as to be disorganizing in itself. But the process by which change takes place and is met influences families as much, perhaps, as the fact of change itself.

One influences the process from within the person; this is the objective toward which counseling and educational services frequently aim. However, the attitudes of poor people are an adjustive response to what goes on around them. A constructive process of change must be developed around the families. . . .

In considering community services, we shall be touching on the techniques of block organization and citizen participation in urban renewal. Though these activities may arise from different sources, they have a common core in the notion that people want to govern themselves. Urban renewal can succeed without such activities—at a cost. That is—

. . . by creating a wide gulf between the aims of renewal and the interests of citizens, it is likely that such renewal programs will radically transform the neighborhood composition, leading to ironic results in which a renewed neighborhood may have lost the population for which it was being renewed.

Without participation, the poor would have moved on. On the other hand, if permitted or shown the way, they may act on their own behalf. It should be evident that such activities set their sights on the poor individual's feeling of importance. (Perhaps "you *can* fight City Hall!" And what if City Hall is working with you!) There are communities in which impressive results have been reported.

. . .

If we truly rebuild for the poor, we shall have quite a different approach to many areas. The advice of poor people would be sought, not only as therapy for them but also because they are the clients of the architect and the city planner. . . . Poor people might be engaged—an expensive process, no doubt—in the manual rebuilding of their neighborhoods as, experimentally, they have been engaged in building a number of playgrounds. . . . Proposals that some percentage of units in cleared areas be reserved for low-income tenancy would carry new weight. One would consider methods to make it feasible for tenants of low-rental housing to remain in them—perhaps to purchase them—as their incomes rise. Such a program should convince poor people that they were the purpose of urban renewal, not pawns in its path. In short, we should seek not only to do for but to do with, and then to live up to the commitments that had been implied. It would be quite different from what we are now doing. Perhaps the degree of difference should lead us to reflect upon our present purposes.

.   .   .

How the Poor are Housed

Analysis . . . of income and new housing in the years 1947 to 1958 shows that it was, on the whole, those families with over $6,000 a year who were served. Families with less than $6,000 account for 88 percent of the substandard housing in the country, suggesting that they are not served very well by existing housing either. Many have adequate housing, especially if they are close to $6,000 income or if the income supports one or two people rather than four or five. But it seems clear that income of at least $6,000 is required to assure adequate family housing. . . . It is evident that the family to which we are addressing our attention, with income equivalent to $2,500 or less for a family of four, will have to make adjustments of some kind in their housing expenditures.

How do poor families pay for housing? The question has dimensions that are private and public. As a private matter, the question is answerable in terms of budget management and family arrangements. As a public matter, one answers in terms of specific public programs or of the concept that housing filters down to the poor as those who are better off move on to better housing. . . .

The Private Dimension

The poor pay for housing, first, in its poor quality. . . . Whether they own or rent, it is the poor families who tend to occupy the country's substandard housing. In 1956 half of those with income less than $2,000 lived in housing that was dilapidated or lacked plumbing.

This is a rough measure. We have not taken into account size of family. Moreover, current income counts several kinds of people as if they were the same: the rich man who has taken a temporary loss, the retired man who once had more income, and the man who is chronically poor. The first man is likely to be able to spend out of savings and conceivably the retired man too, but hardly the man who has never had a decent income. Nevertheless, the rough measure makes it clear that some who are poor acquire standard housing. . . .

One step that poor families take is to allocate a high percentage of their income to housing. . . . In 1956 the great majority of families with incomes under $2,000 spent 30 percent or more of their income on rent. On the other hand, of families with incomes between $8,000 and $10,000 the great majority spent less than 15 percent. . . .

What would a suitable yardstick be? For most cities the BLS city worker's family budget allocates to housing something less than 20 percent of the total. Moreover, the BLS budget totals are over twice as high as the level of poverty. One would assume that if, out of incomes already lower than adequate, more than 20 percent is allocated to housing, increased deprivation will be felt in other areas of the budget. . . .

One possibility is clear—to pay for adequate shelter by settling for inadequate food and clothing. In many cases, the family must be governed not by a deliberate choice to favor housing but by the way inadequate money gets spent. Under sustained pressure, costs that are fixed and regular are met

and those that seem stretchable or postponable—food, clothing, recreation, medical care—are not met. In any case, the
consequences of spending more than 20 percent for housing
do not seem healthy.

. . .

The strategies that are open to poor families are not limited
to trying to shift small sums of money. Analysis of the living
arrangements of the aged in the United States indicates that,
when help for the old person is needed, the poor tend to pool
living arrangements. The plight of the poor "is so difficult
that they must select the most efficient way of sharing, which
is living together." An attempt to understand crowding among
Negroes in Chicago produces a somewhat similar observation.

. . .

As a private matter, then, poor families get and apply
money wherever they can. They use a variety of strategies,
some because they come to hand and some in which there
is a measure of choice. An aged widow will make different
adjustments from a young father, for example. But few of
the deliberate choices that are open seem attractive. Families
can go without standard housing. They can borrow from food
to pay housing. Few who are poor will have saved money;
those who have, can use it. They can struggle to buy on
credit or to borrow. They can try to buy instead of rent. Those
who manage to bring this off may make out better in the
end. Others will face additional difficulty because they are
borrowing from other budget items and are leaving themselves less room to maneuver in the next emergency. They
can extend the size of their households, trading crowded-
ness and tension for shelter and a measure of financial
flexibility. Families can break up or at least give up children.
Throughout, they can seek ways to improve their income.
Some poor families try all of these. For some but not for
others, purchasing a house and sending additional members
to work . . . are constructive steps. For the rest of it, the
avenues that are open go around in a tight little circle, en-
meshing families deeper and deeper in deprivation.

. . .

The Public Dimension

. . . Public housing is not available to more than a small proportion of the low-income families. Though the Housing Act of 1949 authorized 810,000 units, that authorization is as yet far from exhausted. There are in all something over half a million units—roughly 1 percent of the housing supply. If public housing were limited to the lowest incomes, with current resources it could house 2 million of the 32 million . . . poor. As it reaches above the very lowest incomes, it houses even a smaller percentage of the poor than these figures indicate. Consequently there are waiting lists of people eligible for public housing. In the District of Columbia, the number of families awaiting admission has at times exceeded the total number of housing units.

. . . The bulk of families entering public housing have incomes under $4,000 a year. Among the families having less than $4,000, in the total population roughly one in four has under $1,500 income. But only one in eight of those who move into public housing has less than $1,500.†

. . . When they are asked, the majority of families who live in public housing say that they like it. They appreciate its facilities; their general morale is higher than it was in substandard housing. One must, of course, take into account that those who would object most to public housing never enter it, or they leave.‡ Nevertheless, for those who take up tenancy, public housing represents a considerable improvement in physical surroundings. Moreover, the aspects of the environment which are offensive to some families may be secondary or even functional for others.

. . . Public housing performs at least acceptably for those poor families who see it as an improved, somewhat protected

† Perhaps half of the families with less than $1,500 income who move into public housing are public assistance recipients. The non-recipient with very low income is therefore represented in a very small proportion indeed.

‡ The rate of moveouts, though it signals difficulty in some places, is not strikingly high compared with general population mobility. It is lower over-all than the moveout rate for rental housing insured by FHA.

environment. Presumably, it offers their children a better start than they might otherwise have had. Analysis of turnover statistics suggests that others use public housing as a way station to improved housing. In this sense, too, public housing serves the prevention of poverty.

PUBLIC ASSISTANCE

. . . At the beginning of 1962, over 7-million people were receiving assistance. Though less directly than public housing, to be sure, public assistance is the largest national program concerned with the housing needs of the poor. It is important, therefore, to ask about the quality of housing that assistance recipients secure and about the welfare department's influence upon it.

Although information about the quality of recipients' housing has not been systematically collected, it is clear that the quality is poor. Data about plumbing facilities . . . suggest how the housing of recipients compares with that of the general population. It may not be surprising that assistance recipients, having the lowest incomes, are worse off than the average. However, it is an impressive figure that 4 out of 10 aged recipients and 3 out of 19 recipient families with dependent children manage without each of these basic facilities. One can guess at the proportions of their dwellings that are dilapidated and deteriorated. Measures of crowding suggest that over-time assistance recipients are not improving their housing at the same rate as the general population. . . .

Special State and city studies provide a more intimate appraisal of the housing of public assistance recipients. Florida reviewed 13,000 cases of aid to families with dependent children to determine whether the homes were suitable for children. The study noted "excessively high rents for unspeakably inadequate slum homes." A survey of recipient families with dependent children in the State of Maine found that four out of five did not have central heating. . . . And

none of all 3 of the essential plumbing facilities: running
water, bath and exclusive use of toilet. . . .

Can Poor Families be Housed?

If one reflects upon the ways in which poor families pay
for housing in their private lives and upon the ways in which
public policies assist them, it is possible to perceive a discrepancy. The private and the public dimensions are out of
balance. Poor people pay for housing as a total effort, out of
their food and out of the fabric of their lives together. The
effects of the struggle are experienced without Sabbath and
without holiday. But public efforts to assist them are directed
only to a minority. Out of those who are reached, many are
helped meagerly, subject to conditions that may be relevant,
irrelevant, or even self-defeating.

In public efforts to provide housing we have so far relied
chiefly upon stimulation and subsidy of private industry. The
results, for those with incomes over $5,000 or $6,000, have
been respectable. Recent legislation attempts to extend the
impact of such activity to lower incomes. The problem has so
far appeared to be one of interesting builders and developers
in such a market. It appears likely that some gains will be
made. But it must be evident that the problem of the poor will
not be met in this manner. We have referred to the reasons;
they require only to be brought together.

First, though special incentives for low-income building
and contraction of demand in the middle-income market may
lead to more builder interest in low-cost housing than heretofore, it is unlikely that interest will reach down to the families with $2,500 incomes. High risks, limited profits, and
other difficulties that have discouraged business from building for families with $5,000 incomes will seem insuperable at
half those incomes.

Second, it is not unreasonable that builders and banks
should take pause. A family of four with less than $2,500
income is not able to buy a house or pay a rent that provides a
profit on it, no matter how low the interest rate on the mort-

gage. The family's income is not adequate to its need for food, clothing, and other necessary items—even if it were paying no rent at all.

Third, inducing low-income families to pay 25 or 30 percent of their incomes carries a heavy risk of its own and is not sound public policy. The housing that is bought at the expense of food or medical care is dearly bought.

This is not to say that we are unable to provide decent housing for all American families. Public housing and public assistance provide avenues for decent housing, providing that the serious limitations of these programs are corrected. Small-scale experiments of other sorts are being tried. A number involve public subsidy to those who provide housing for low-income families, with purchasers or tenants making such payments as they can afford. There has been recurrent consideration of the possibility of providing a direct subsidy to low-income families to be used for purchasing or renting standard housing. Such a proposal was considered by Senator Robert A. Taft. Reporting in 1945, the subcommittee rejected direct subsidies, mainly because they might flow to substandard housing. There was also objection to channeling such funds through public assistance agencies. After more than a decade of experience with urban renewal, attention has been turning again to the possibility of providing a direct subsidy to poor families. A number of schemes have been put forward that provide protections against misuse; nor would subsidies necessarily be furnished through public assistance agencies. . . .

Poverty and the Administration of Justice in the Criminal Courts

JUNIUS L. ALLISON

In a recent issue of *The New Yorker* there is a very readable profile on "Our Invisible Poor," in which Dwight Macdonald reviews several current books on poverty.

. . .

The New Yorker article suggests that today it is easy for the poor to slip out of the "experience and consciousness of the nation"—to become *invisible*. (1) The poor are usually isolated and out of sight, in the central area of the city. (2) Clothes make the poor invisible—since it is easier to dress decently than it is to be decently housed or fed or even doctored. (3) Many are of the wrong age to be seen—too old or too young. (4) Finally, a great percentage are politically invisible—no lobbies, no legislative program. . . .

The indigent person whose rights are often ignored in the tangled processes of the law is quite *visible* and quite significant in a society that boasts of *equality before the law*.

. . .

. . . How can we safeguard the rights of the poor, the ignorant, the inarticulate, the frightened, and the insecure without becoming too paternalistic in demanding standards of conduct, or by placing exacting restrictions upon the way

§ Junius L. Allison, "Poverty and the Administration of Justice in the Criminal Courts," reprinted by special permission of *The Journal of Criminal Law, Criminology and Police Science,* vol. 55, no. 2, pp. 241–245 (copyright © 1964 by the Northwestern University School of Law).

they use their vitamins, their priviliges, their education, and how they occupy their place in the sun?

Consider the recent controversies over the treatment of recipients of ADC in some areas.

1. In three New Jersey counties mothers of illegitimate children have been prosecuted under otherwise unenforced adultery and fornication laws.
2. In Connecticut, an attempt was made to "deport" a mother of an illegitimate child, both of whom were receiving public assistance. The Legal Aid Society successfully challenged the constitutionality of the action.
3. Recently in Alameda County, for the purpose of discovering a "man in the house," night raids (without search warrants) were made in the homes of 500 mothers who were receiving support for their needy children. This has been repeated, on a less comprehensive scope, in many other jurisdictions.

A law professor at Yale University writes that "it has become common practice for authorities to make unannounced inspections of homes of persons receiving public assistance."

Where do we draw the line between the constitutional right of equal treatment, right of free movement, right of privacy, *on the one hand,* and what must be the responsibility of the state to spend the taxpayer's dollar wisely and effectively, *on the other*?

Another situation that shows a dramatic by-product of poverty involves the indigent defendant who is held in jail preceding his trial. This confinement can be days, weeks, or even months for those unable to make bond. In the federal courts and in many states, this period of incarceration is not credited against any subsequent sentence. If the accused is ultimately acquitted, the unfortunate predicament is made more tragic.

For instance, according to the Mayor's Committee, in 1960, a total of 114,653 persons were detained in New York City jails. Yet only 30,827 defendants were later sentenced to prison terms. Another study showed that 28 per cent of the defendants were too poor to post bond where the bail was set at $500 and 45 per cent could not raise bail when it was set at $2,000.

Forty-six thousand persons were sentenced in New York City in 1961, but 118,000 had been held in jail, some for as long as six months, most of them being unable to make bail.

In 1961 the Vera Foundation launched the Manhattan Bail Project in cooperation with the New York University School of Law and the Institute of Judicial Administration. This study was to test the hypothesis that a greater number of defendants could be successfully released on their own recognizance if verified information about them, their families, and their roots in the community were presented to the court.

Under the procedure followed in this project, a prisoner is interviewed between the time of arrest and arraignment. At present the experiment does not cover defendants charged with narcotic offenses, homicide, forcible rape, or offenses against a minor. Five principal plus-factors are given great weight in deciding whether a defendant is a likely parole risk: present or recent residence at same address for six months, current or recent job for six months, relatives in New York City, no previous conviction, and residence in New York City for ten years or more.

In the first year more than 275 defendants were released on the basis of information furnished the court. Only three persons jumped parole. Of the first hundred parolees, 60 were ultimately acquitted; 30 were given suspended sentences, six were fined, and four drew prison terms. During the first month of the Project, 25 per cent of those interviewed were found to qualify for pretrial parole; nine months later about 50 percent of those studied were recommended as good prospects.†

† In a more recent report made by Herbert Sturz, Executive Director of the Vera Foundation . . . , we are told that during the first two years of the Project, of the more than 800 defendants released on their

The most ironic finding in the whole study is the revelation that accused persons whom the law presumes to be innocent, are confined pending trial under conditions which are more oppressive and restrictive than those applied to convicted and sentenced felons. Our appellate courts have reinforced the philosophy that we abhor the imposition of criminal sanctions before the accused is convicted. It is surprising to learn that under the usually harsh law of early England, an indigent could obtain bail more easily than he can today.

This New York experiment is a very positive and real approach to a serious problem that exists in every criminal court. It is encouraging to know that the Project will be continued. It has just received a grant of $115,000 from the Ford Foundation. There is little doubt that the final results of the study will be valuable to other jurisdictions. Indeed, one Chicago judge has already established a similar practice in his court. I feel certain that we are to hear much more about this innovation in the somewhat sick bail system that now exists to sustain the professional bondsmen and penalize the poor.

The third and last issue I wish to raise in regard to poverty and the administration of our criminal law is one that arouses an even greater interest among lawyers. It is the right to have the assistance of counsel when one is accused of a violation of the law.

I need not labor the point that a lay person, even an educated one, needs a lawyer when his life or his liberty is at stake in a criminal proceeding. . . .

The constitutional guarantees of the right to have counsel provided for indigent defendants are reasonably comprehensive. Under the sixth amendment the Court has said that unless counsel is waived, indigent defendants in *federal courts* must have legal assistance provided. In applying the due process clause of the fourteenth amendment to actions in

own recognizance, upon recommendation of Vera staff members, 99 per cent returned to court as required. Mr. Sturz also reports that similar experiments are being started in St. Louis, Chicago, Washington, D.C., and Baltimore.

state courts, the Supreme Court, since the time of the *Scottsboro* case, has ruled that in every capital case, counsel must be made available and, since 1942, has held that for those charged with non-capital felonies, counsel must be provided if the presence of the defense lawyer is necessary for a fair trial.

And now, in a case handed down on March 18th, 1963, the Supreme Court . . . held that under the due process clause of the fourteenth amendment a defendant in any serious case has an absolute right of counsel. This will place a greater administrative responsibility on the states which heretofore did not, as a matter of course, provide lawyers for the indigent defendants. It will bring greater pressure for the adoption of some organized plan to meet the situation.

Fortunately, there were only 12 states . . . whose laws or rules did not require the appointment of counsel in all felony cases without regard to "special circumstances." Of these, the five southern states, Alabama, Florida, Mississippi, North Carolina, and South Carolina, are the least concerned with the right to have the assistance of counsel. (However, since the decision in *Gideon,* Florida has added 12 public defenders and North Carolina has provided for compensating counsel for indigent defendants charged with felonies.)

The practical administrative problem of *how* to provide counsel presents a far more controversial question than the philosophical one concerning the *right* to have representation. Under the traditional method, the trial judge appoints a lawyer from a volunteer panel or designates an attorney who happens to be in the court room at the time the accused is arraigned. Such an informal arrangement worked fairly well in rural America where the volume of cases was small and every lawyer was a general practitioner, including the prosecuting attorney. However, with the growth of our large cities and the specialization of law practice, the long criminal docket has presented a more difficult problem for the metropolitan centers.

. . .

The Public Defender idea was first adopted in Oklahoma in

1911 as a solution to the problem of the increasing number of criminal cases in the urban centers. In 1914 this innovation was followed by Los Angeles—a county that has the largest and one of the most effective offices in the country. One-hundred-ten other jurisdictions have established similar services. Under this plan, financial support comes from the city, county, or state. The Public Defender is selected in various ways: by civil service, by the judges, by the county commissioner, or, in a few places, he is elected.

The Private Defender system differs in that funds to support the office come from voluntary sources—such as the bar association, individual contributors, or the United Fund. The NLADA records show 13 cities and counties with Private Defenders.

Then, there is a third type of organization—the mixed Public-Private office that exists in twelve cities. Here an independent society sets the policies and selects the Defender, yet part of the funds come from the county or municipality.

There are, of course, weaknesses and strengths in each of these systems. Each has strong and persuasive advocates among the bar and judiciary.

Regardless of individual preferences concerning the various organizations, the total number of cases handled each year is substantial and the cost is surprisingly low. The 1962 statistics gathered by the NLADA show that about 142,000 indigent defendants were represented at an average cost of approximately $19 per case. Further, there is reason to believe that in most instances the representation is competent. As one example, we note that the annual report of the Public Defender of Cook County shows that last year the office obtained acquittals for 52 per cent of the defendants tried before juries or before the court.

Unfortunately, there are many large cities that have no organized Defender services. Almost one-half of the 136 offices are located in California and Illinois. Thirty-four states have no such offices at all. There are 34 counties of more than 400,000 population each where only the haphazard appointment system exists.

In the federal courts, the problem is even more acute. Since there are no paid Defenders and no funds to compensate counsel appointed by the court, the lawyers must volunteer their services, pay for investigation, and bear all other out-of-pocket expenses. For the past 20 years efforts have been made to provide compensation for lawyers representing indigent defendants in the federal courts. The Judicial Conference has urged this legislation on at least 17 occasions, and it has been supported by every United States Attorney General since 1937. In February, 1963, the American Bar Association adopted a strong resolution calling for Congressional action.

Legislation has passed the Senate three times, but the Judiciary Committee of the House has held up the bills each year. Fortunately, the picture is brighter now. With the full and active support of the ABA and many state bar associations we expect the passage of some favorable legislation.

S. 1057 . . . embodies most of the ABA recommendations.† Principal among these are the alternative provisions permitting a federal district to adopt one of four methods of compensating counsel for indigent defendants:

a. Public Defender,
b. A bar association service, Legal Aid Society, or use of an existing state Defender system.
c. Compensation of private counsel on a case-by-case method.
d. Any combination of these.

It is indeed a strange contradiction we have in the federal system, where, on one hand, the Constitution gives everyone the right to have a lawyer, requiring that one be provided if the defendant is poor, and, on the other, having no provision for compensating or reimbursing the hundreds of lawyers who serve when they are appointed. With the some 35,000 federal cases each year—one-third to one-half being indigent—this problem is more than academic. The legal pro-

† S. 1057 became Public Law 88–455 on August 20, 1964.

fession and the public generally are faced with a situation so serious that it is threatening the administration of justice in a branch of our court system that we regard as the most efficient, the fairest, and the best organized. . . .

(23)

Poverty and Health

ROBERT L. EICHHORN AND
EDWARD G. LUDWIG

HEALTH CHANCES

Health is basically a matter of chance, the chance of warding off disease, the chance of detecting it and the chance of recovery from its ravages. In an age which knew little about the causes of disease and much less about its treatment, disease and death did not discriminate. The rich and the poor suffered alike. Today, however, money can buy health and does so for millions through inoculations, medicines, surgical operations and vacations. How long a person will live, the disease he will have, the type of treatment he will receive, and the cause of his death are all strongly influenced by the amount of money there is to spend on health. While public and private arrangements have been made to provide the poor with the same quality of medical care that the more wealthy can afford, statistics on death and disease show that such efforts have not succeeded. Low

§ Robert Eichhorn and Edward Ludwig, Sociology Department, Purdue University. Reading is previously unpublished.

income still decreases the likelihood of ready access to medical care, freedom from disease and long life.

POVERTY AND DEATH

Since the turn of the century, the average length of life for Americans has increased dramatically as a consequence of a higher standard of living, including more and better health care. At present the newly-born can expect to live nearly 70 years. Yet this average disguises important differences, some very definitely tied to family income. For instance, Negro children born in 1960 will die about eight years sooner than white children.

In the poorest county in the nation with a median income of $1260, 24 percent of the deaths in 1962 were of infants less than one year old, while infant deaths contributed only 6 percent of the deaths for the country as a whole. Infant and neonatal mortality rates among the nonwhite population are twice those of the white population. Death rates among nonwhite infants are nearly three times greater for tuberculosis, six times greater for dysentery, three times greater for measles, two times greater for vascular lesions, almost five times greater for influenza and pneumonia, two times greater for bronchitis, and three times greater for infections of the newborn. Childbirth is also more likely to result in death for poor women.

Infectious diseases, which can generally be stopped short of death, continue to take their toll beyond infancy in the poorer parts of the nation. In rural Mississippi, Arkansas, and Alabama where median family income falls below $4000, chances of dying of tuberculosis and other infectious or parasitic diseases are roughly twice as great as they are in rural Illinois and New York where farm families earn median incomes above $6000. Within the single city of New York, death rates from tuberculosis, influenza, and pneumonia are significantly higher in those health districts having a preponderance of low-income families.

At any age death rates for nonwhites compare unfavorably with those of whites for both infectious and degenerative diseases. During childhood the death rate among nonwhites for rheumatic heart disease is four times greater than that for whites. In early adulthood, the death rate is six times greater for rheumatic heart disease, five times greater for chronic endocarditis, and eight times greater for influenza and pneumonia. Among nonwhites in middle adulthood, the death rates for vascular lesions, diabetes and tuberculosis are all at least four times greater. And in the later years when chronic diseases begin to loom more importantly as a cause of death, nonwhites are twice as likely to die of malignant neoplasms and of diseases of the cardiovascular system.

POVERTY AND SICKNESS

But statistics on death tell only part of the story. The poor are likely to experience more sickness during their lifetime, acute episodes and chronic conditions, and mental illness as well.

According to National Health Survey data collected from noninstitutionalized persons during a single year in the early 1960's, about 81 million persons in the United States, representing 45 percent of the population have one or more chronic conditions. These range from comparatively minor disorders such as sinusitis or hay fever to heart disease and diabetes. But chronic conditions which interfere with one's usual daily activities are concentrated among the poor: 60 percent of those with incomes below $2000 compared to 24 percent of those above $7000 are limited in their activities by their disorder. Three times as many people per 1000 in a given year are at home recovering from some chronic ailment among families with less than $4000 than among those with more. Any one of the common chronic diseases (heart conditions, arthritis and rheumatism, mental and nervous disorders, high blood pressure) interfere most with the customary activities of the poor.

Americans suffer slightly over two episodes of acute disease in the course of a year. These include infectious and parasitic diseases, respiratory conditions, and injuries. The higher one's family income, the more likely he will have some acute ailment: digestive diseases are the exception. However, conditions that neither restricted activity nor received medical attention were excluded, and one suspects that the poor may be less likely to define an acute illness particularly among their children as demanding special attention. For after the age of 15, acute conditions are consistently more prevalent among the poor, a difference that increases with age.

Chronic and acute conditions together result in twice as many days of restricted activity for those with family incomes under $2000 as for those making over $7000. This amounts to 30 lost days a year. The poor spend twice the number of days confined to their beds, one-fifth more days in the hospital, nearly twice the days away from work and a somewhat greater number of days out of school because of illness. The vicious circle is complete: the poor lose more time from productive activity because of illness, which in turn deprives them of the income necessary to improve their health through better food, more adequate housing, and preventive and corrective medical care.

MEDICAL SERVICES, COSTS AND FINANCING

Nearly three-fourths of the people in the United States have some form of health insurance coverage. This plus state and local public assistance programs convey an impression of blanket and ample protection for all and serves to obscure the fact that those most in need of medical services are least likely to receive them.

Of persons with a family income of less than $2000, only 34 percent have some type of hospital or surgical insurance, often with quite limited benefits. Those with large families are especially vulnerable: among the well-to-do, large and small families are about equally covered, but 47 percent of the small, poor families are covered by health insurance compared to 15 percent of the larger ones. The aged, who experience more illness and are most likely to have limited income, are also less likely to have health insurance, since health insurance is generally a fringe benefit offered by the better companies to the regularly employed. As a result of these several factors, health insurance pays *no part* of the hospital bill in 60 percent of the cases of persons from families with incomes under $2000 compared to 19 percent from those with incomes above $7000.

Public assistance is intended to help those who cannot provide for themselves. But public assistance in the form of financial aid or medical services can be no more adequate in meeting health needs than the wealth of the state, county or city permits. Even in the wealthy metropolitan areas, public assistance for medical care is usually skimpy and erratic. According to legislative determination, a person may qualify for aid by virtue of his blindness, regardless of financial need, but not for an infected kidney. Or he may be called upon to prove that he cannot pay for a specific service, which tends to limit the type of care he receives to emergencies, excluding diagnostic and preventive care.

Means tests were designed to eliminate all but the needy from seeking public assistance and to conserve limited funds for medical care. At present, one half of the states utilizing the Medical Aid for the Aged Program (Kerr-Mills Act), restrict eligibility to persons with incomes below $1200, and two-thirds of the states exclude couples with assets over $1500. In practice the older person is asked to sacrifice what little security he has remaining for much needed medical care. Among a generation of proud folk who have been taught frugality, self-reliance and planning for the future, it is not uncommon for many to forego medical assistance rather than give up the meager assets they possess.

Some regions of the United States are medically impoverished, and even health insurance or public assistance cannot purchase services that do not exist. C. Horace Hamilton found that 96 of 190 counties in Southern Appalachia have no health officer of any kind. Physicians practicing in these poor rural areas tend to be old and overworked. An only physician in a county of 6100 may see in his office forty patients a day, seven days a week. There may be no hospital in the county. The shortage of physicians and adequate medical facilities is a problem not limited to rural areas: the situation is also desperate in the urban slums.

These impediments to adequate medical care impose their penalty upon the poor. Low income families see their doctor less often each year than the more favored: families with incomes under $4000 average 4.6 visits a year compared to 5.7 visits for those earning more. The poor encounter the doctor in the hospital clinic, while others more often meet him in his office or contact him by phone. . . . The poor are less likely to use the services of the specialists, such as pediatricians, obstetricians, ophthalmologists and the like. Their surgeons are less frequently board certified, and surgery itself is less common. The poor have fewer X-rays taken, and those they have are more often taken in the hospital rather than in the doctor's office. Seventy-eight percent of those earning less than $2000 compared to 42 percent with a family income of $7000 fail to see a dentist during a given year. The need for fillings, cleaning and straightening generally take the economically favored to the dentist, while the need for extractions and denture work motivate the poor.

The economically deprived as a group go to the hospital less often. However, those who must go are likely to be admitted more than once a year, to remain for a longer period of time, and require more time for convalescence. All indicate delay in seeking proper medical attention. That limited income serves as a barrier to the poor was shown by the national surveys of the Health Information Foundation: the hospital admission rate is highest among low income persons *covered by insurance.*

The poor spend less for hospitals, doctors, dentists and medicine than those with higher family incomes. This amounted to $112 per person for those families earning under $2000 in 1962 contrasted to $153 for those with incomes over $7000. Yet this smaller amount represents a larger proportion of disposable income. Thirty percent of the low income families spent nothing for medical services during the preceding twelve months, compared to 11 percent of the high income families. The economically deprived are most likely to do without or to make do with a cheaper substitute, resorting to patent medicine or folk remedies.

While dollars and cents may have initially prevented the poor from getting the medical care they need, money alone will not right the situation. There has developed a *culture of poverty* that includes health, making legitimate certain unsound health practices which are extremely resistant to change.

THE CULTURE OF POVERTY AND HEALTH

Poverty is a way of life based upon shared experiences, knowledge, values and expectations for the future. Consequently, the poor regard matters of sickness and health differently from the wealthy as they do the importance of education or family size.

The very definition of illness itself is different from one income group to another, a crucial factor since it will determine when the person enters the treatment cycle in the first instance. Koos reported that less than one-fifth of the lower class think of chronic fatigue or persistent backache as symptoms worth mentioning to a doctor. He quoted one lower class woman:

"I'd look silly wouldn't I, going to the doctor for a backache. My mother always had a backache as long as I can remember and didn't do anything about it. It didn't kill her, either. If I went to the doctor for that, my friends would hoot me out of town."

Only about one-half recognizes excessive vaginal bleeding

as a reason for concern. Loss of appetite will be ignored by 80 percent of the lower class, fainting spells by 67 percent, and continued coughing by 77 percent.

This lack of concern of the poor for medically significant symptoms rests, in part, upon lack of information. Surveys by the National Opinion Research Center have shown that poorer people are less informed about the symptoms of cancer, diabetes and poliomyelitis. Others have found that the poor do not readily recognize psychological problems, and when they do, they draw a hard-and-fast line between normality and being "nuts" or "crazy." But it is also true that the poor have become stoical about illness, perhaps from necessity, and are prepared to accept some aches and pains. The poor person needs to be a great deal sicker before he or his associates accept him as sick. This delays his visit to a doctor and rules out preventive medicine. It accounts, in part, for his eventual longer stay in the hospital and prolonged period of recuperation following surgery.

Once a person has accepted the fact that he is sick and in need of assistance, he may not necessarily take himself to competent medical personnel. Instead, he may seek the services of a practitioner of folk medicine, a chiropractor or the corner druggist. Koos found that 58 percent of the lower class, compared to two percent of the upper class, would use the chiropractor for *any* illness. They would seek his aid for colds, sore throats, female disorders and heart disease. Customers sometimes force druggists into practicing medicine by prescribing drugs and remedies, the poor being specially prone to do this. The poor also treat themselves. Their medicine chest is especially likely to contain "kidney pills," "liver pills," "stomach tonics" and "blood builders," selected by themselves from the druggist's shelf or recommended, concocted or loaned by others.

On the other hand, the lower income person who does make it to a competent physician is likely to get differential treatment. He is often treated with the thought in mind of saving him some money. Therefore, he is less likely to be advised to undergo extensive diagnosis, less likely to be kept from work, hospitalized or given surgery. Mental illness among the poor is more often treated by therapies disapproved by dynamically-oriented psychiatrists, such as shock, drugs, lobotomies, and custodial care which actually is no treatment at all.

Ironically, the poor would be the last to suspect that their treatment was not the best or, at least, not the most sensible available. Their knowledge of disease is in accord with the treatment they receive. They express faith in tonics which implies a simple cause-effect relationship, and in doctors who do not confuse them. To be put in the hospital or sent home to rest will hardly endear a doctor to a patient who has to work to pay this week's rent.

BREAKING THE LINK BETWEEN POVERTY AND DISEASE

Low income families have less chance to enjoy long life, freedom from disease and ready access to the medical care that would keep them well. Poor health, in turn, perpetuates poverty. Families in which the breadwinner is disabled lose on the average over $3000 in annual income. But the penalties of sickness for the poor go far beyond those measured in dollars and cents: there is also the anxiety, marital conflict and premature death of loved ones. And the foundation for continued poverty is laid when children are forced to drop out of school to enter the labor market without skill in order to supplement family income. Or children marry early to escape a home made unhappy by chronic illness. Therefore, one attack upon poverty should be better medical care for the nation's poor. Broadened programs for preventive and restorative medicine are long overdue.

Psychiatrists and the Poor

ROBERT COLES, M.D.

They live not far from a fine old Carolina city . . . a large tenant farming family whose little girl used to travel many miles to a Negro school, passing other suitable schools on the way.

. . . I spent a number of days with them and at the same time visited a nearby white family. . . . scarcely unlike them in occupation, income, education, and other categories which describe how lives are spent and sometimes squandered. When I left I had gained some interesting information about how children manage—and, in this case, manage well —in difficult and changing times. I had discovered other circumstances, however, which were harder for me to accept.

The girl's father drank heavily and was often exceedingly cruel to his wife and children. Sometimes he would be pleasant enough, but at other times he became sullen and withdrawn. Though poorly educated, he was natively a bright man and certainly a shrewd one. He had seen a local doctor about a year earlier and told him that he felt himself ill mentally, a significant disclosure for him and one which distinguishes him from many others who would not know enough or care enough to do even that. The doctor gave him what he called, as he showed them to me, "quieting pills." They were strong tranquilizers, and they were prescribed with a message: they were all he could expect, given where he lived, his race, his class, his income. "I can't afford much

§ Robert Coles, "Psychiatrists and the Poor," reprinted from *The Atlantic Monthly*, July 1964, pp. 102–106, by permission of the author.

to buy these pills, so I treats them like the gold they looks to be [they are orange-colored], and I uses them for real bad times."

What struck me and troubled me was that this man was really a rather responsive human being, with problems not too hard to fathom and easier to treat than many I have seen. Moreover, his discouraging predicament was shared by the mother of a white boy in the same school with his daughter. With five young children, she was intelligent enough and earnest enough to be ambitious for them, for their health and education. Still, with her concern, with her hard work and zealous pride in her home and family went a severe, a crippling kind of migraine. For days she would be nearly bedridden, and the consequent chaos, it seemed to me, set the stage for a recovery destined all too soon to give way to an anxious, depressed recurrence of illness. She needed better medical care than she was getting; aspirin was simply not the answer for the kind of pain she suffered. She also needed and could make good use of psychiatric care. Her husband knew this, too. One day, while talking of racial matters in the county, he slipped into another vein: "One thing both races lack equally here is good doctoring care for those who need it and want it bad."

There are also those who need medical or psychiatric care and would not dream of asking for it. Yet, if we are to reach these people—and, given sensible planning in a rich country, we should aim to do just that—we will have to keep in mind what I once heard a public health doctor say about some Negro sharecroppers: "We can cure their infections, but I'd hate to have to know what they're thinking."

Psychiatrists have to know a lot about what their patients are thinking and about what they themselves are thinking. . . .

Psychiatrists should not be particularly blamed for their predominantly middle-class clientele or for their increasing concern with the certification of their position in medical centers and wealthy suburbs. . . . Whatever general criticism can be made of them is also applicable to others in

American professional life. Lawyers are now beginning to see how hard it is for the poor to obtain "equal protection under the law," and for the first time our highest courts are prodding them in this regard. Educators are troubled by their failure to reach millions of potentially educable, even gifted children. The fact that money purchases the best medical care and that the want of it frequently consigns one to the worst is a fact of life throughout the nation. When psychiatric goods and services follow similar patterns of distribution, they are simply conforming to the way our society is set up.

. . .

. . . Three major studies . . . stand out as landmarks: the Yale study by A. Hollingshead and F. C. Redlich of the relationship between social class and mental illness, and the two studies which have come from the social psychiatry unit of the Cornell Medical School—the Stirling County Study of Psychiatric Disorder and Sociocultural Environment and the Midtown Manhattan Study, whose findings were published in book form under the title *Mental Health in the Metropolis.* These carefully documented researches have all been concerned with the relationship of class—social and economic background—to mental illness, and with the incidence of mental illness in cities and towns. What we learn from these reports is revealing about psychiatrists, their patients, and our society. . . .

The Yale study, published under the title *Social Class and Mental Illness,* concerns itself with the relationship between social class and both psychiatric symptoms and care, and is a sociological and psychiatric study of New Haven. It was done with scrupulous concern for statistical validity. The class structure of the city was analyzed and described. The patterns of mental illness and its treatment are shown. The book reveals that poor people tend to have a higher incidence of diagnosed psychoses, the most serious form of mental disease, and also receive radically different forms of medical and psychiatric care for their difficulties. Whereas the wealthy and the well-to-do are more likely to be treated with individual psychotherapy, purchased privately or secured at clinics which largely provide for the middle classes, the poor are usually sent to hospitals and, once there, receive the less humane treatment of electric shock or drugs.

The authors of the Yale study are not content merely to emphasize these cold-blooded facts and the influence of money on psychiatric diagnoses and treatment. They examine the interesting relationship of the psychiatrist, as a middle-class citizen, to the large number of poor patients he may be called to see and subsequently—persuaded by forces in his own life—reject or diagnose in ways reflecting more about his life than their illness. . . . An infection is an infection, and rich or poor respond to the same dosage of penicillin. Mental illness is not so easy to treat, and the psychiatrist cannot depend upon pills, vaccines, or intravenous solutions, all nicely free of biases of personality and prejudices of class.

In a sense, most of the findings of the Yale study confirm the difficult problems of psychiatry as a profession under heavy demands in American life. . . . As Redlich and Hollingshead point out at the end of their book, there are too few good therapists, meeting all too many patients; the poor, the culturally or socially exiled, are frequently hard for many psychiatrists to understand, hence suitably treat; large numbers of patients therefore find their way to those sad and sometimes outrageous back wards of state institutions. Or they may run the risk of inadequate evaluation and hasty, basically faulty treatment. Such are the troubles with which the poor and their society, including its psychiatrists, must cope.

The apathy of the poor needs no psychiatric study for its proof, nor do their widespread dependency, their common lack of tidiness, thrift, and respect for the legal and moral codes embraced by their "betters." What is needed, the Yale investigators emphasize, is careful studies of incidence, of prevalence of disease in communities, of attempted correlation of such occurrence with as large a number of environmental facts as possible. The more we know of the external forces involved in mental illness, the more we understand the obviously complex connection between individual and social pathology

The Cornell unit in social psychiatry has taken up where its brother group in New Haven suggested the need was greatest. Its work is both extensive and impressive. Its intention, exemplified by such studies as the Yorkville one in Manhattan and the Stirling County one in Nova Scotia, has been to find out how many people actually are mentally ill in a large city, or a small town, or a village, and who those people are, by race, religion, occupation, education, marital status, and a host of significant social and economic variables.

One of their crucial findings ties in all too neatly with the Yale study: social disorganization is associated with a significantly higher incidence of mental illness. And, in any case, the incidence of mental illness may well be higher than the statistics indicate. Among the poor it frequently goes unrecorded or unrecognized. Indeed, the gist of the Cornell studies is that psychiatric symptoms bear substantial relationship to various social, cultural, and economic conditions. Worse, among large numbers of poor these symptoms abound and tend to be handed down to children as a kind of grim social inheritance, making it harder and harder for each generation to escape the bondage rising out of the hopelessness and shallowness of life in the rural or city slum.

What these statistics and research studies with their abstractions tell us, all too many testify to in their daily lives— lives hobbled with joblessness, with uselessness, with arbitrary unkindness or contempt at the hands of others. Millions in such straits know constant mental hurt, emotional suffering, despair of the soul without any possibility of help. Their troubles are both real and imaginary—hunger breeds suspicion, hate breeds fear and retaliatory hate—and relief for both kinds of troubles is often inadequate. It is an ironic sorrow for many well-intentioned people in the social sciences that they know these facts and are unable to do much to correct them.

. . .

The irony revealed by both the Yale and Cornell studies is that psychiatrists are frequently out of touch with the conditions which help create their potentially sickest patients. The incidence of paranoid schizophrenia among Negroes is high, probably an example of social reality kindling medical ruin. How many Negroes in the South can go to strictly segregated psychiatric facilities and feel secure and wanted enough to discuss their innermost thoughts and fears? We talk about segregation, by custom, law, or fact; we easily denounce it. A state of affairs which renders a mentally disturbed Negro, wherever he lives, unable to seek or secure competent medical and psychiatric care is a personal tragedy, not an abstract injustice, for millions of individuals—and not the least for the doctors concerned.

I have seen some segregated Negro "state hospitals" in the South, and all too many seriously disturbed Negro children, youths, and adults in Northern cities. The mother of one of the Negro children who is pioneering desegregation in his state had received the care of that state's mental hospital system. Curious, I went there for a visit. She had called the place "that hell." I found her description a bit subdued. The real hell for anyone, especially when troubled, is loneliness. It is hellish to be mentally ill, additionally so to be confined and largely ignored, particularly at the hands of white officials who have little respect for one's basic human dignity. "Maybe I could talk with *some* white doctors; I'm not saying I can't," the mother said, "but I sometimes wonder—and anyway, even if I could, they never have wanted to talk with me." She suffered from periodic depressions, crippling while they lasted. She could be reached, be helped, at least in theory. . . .

Those pockets of poverty whose existence is increasingly acknowledged are also pockets of many kinds of psychopathology, mostly untreated. In some instances—with migratory farm workers, Indians, and many of the Appalachian whites

—the people are not merely poor, not only beyond the reach or even ken of medical or psychiatric attention, but are really striking examples of what social scientists call "subcultures. . . ."

Such people may confuse, then alarm, and finally anger us, doctors included. Their experience has not been ours. We are provoked by their laziness or various forms of easy living. They, in turn, are at a loss to understand, given what is possible for them, what we would have them do. "I tried," a white hillbilly told me, and he repeated the words, "I tried to get a job for a long time here, and then I even went up to Chicago, but there wasn't anything to do, and so we figured we'd rather die here where our kin come from."

There was no question in my mind that two of his children needed the help of a child psychiatrist. One was irritable, still wet the bed at ten, was much too mean to herself (picking at her scalp) and to her all too many brothers and sisters as well. Another child, a boy of twelve, was deeply, deadly, silent and had been so for a long time. . . .

What do they do, these millions of our poor? What happens to their neuroses and psychoses? They live with them and die with them or of them. In cities violence, vagrancy, alcoholism, addiction, apathy, high suicide rates, high murder rates, high delinquency rates bespeak the hopelessness which becomes depression, the doubts which become paranoia, the confusions which become addiction, the frantic attempt to make sense of a senseless world which becomes drunkenness or sudden irrational ferocity. In rural areas, on farms or reservations, the same human scene can be found: retarded children, epileptic children kept, and their limitations accepted, not as possible challenges to be overcome, but as the grim reminders of an all-too-familiar fate; disgruntled, liquored parents venting their frustrations and discouragement in angry feuds and spells of silence or inaction which in many of us would warrant immediate hospitalization.

. . .

The solutions to some of these problems will come in part with the recognition of them, followed by laws which authorize more money and more trained personnel to deal with them. As for the problem of the limited relationship between psychiatrists and some of the neediest of our mentally ill, the Yale and Cornell studies emphasize the necessity to look closely at the training of psychiatrists and those in associated professions. They suggest changes in training programs, a fresh look at how to get more suitably trained and better motivated recruits.

Some of their recommendations are to a limited extent being followed by recent federal legislation on mental retardation and mental health. Others are a direct challenge to several professions to look at their work and their ideals, to free themselves of certain rigidities of thought, to make themselves more responsive to critical needs.

Yet, even with more planning and some new professional flexibility from social scientists, there will remain serious problems for both the poor and our American psychiatrists.

.   .   .

The poor neither know about us nor can they afford our expensive care. And often we do not know about the poor and seem little concerned about getting to know them. These are the facts, plain to see but not so easy to change. Nevertheless, the medical profession and its several specialties will have to serve the large numbers who need them most and can afford them least. To do this will require effort in changing curricula and effort in living up to the old but sometimes forgotten ideals of what a doctor should be. The Yale study is even more explicit: doctors largely come with middle-class views when they approach the poor and usually have little interest in going beyond those views, many of them unsympathetic or outright antagonistic to lower-class people and their kind of living. I have seen many bright young men and women who will never get to college, let alone medical school, because of who they are and their environmental handicaps.

Some of them might become doctors and psychiatrists if they could get financial assistance and continue their education. And then they might help their own people and their profession to achieve an urgently needed mutual understanding.

((25))

Two Case Studies

AUGUST P. HOLLINGSHEAD AND
FREDERICK C. REDLICH

Case histories of two compulsively promiscuous adolescent females . . . illustrate the differential impact of class status on the way in which lay persons and psychiatrists perceive and appraise similar behavior. Both girls came to the attention of the police at about the same time but under very different circumstances. One came from a core group class I family, the other from a class V family broken by the desertion of the father. The class I girl, after one of her frequent drinking and sexual escapades on a weekend away from an exclusive boarding school, became involved in an automobile accident while drunk. Her family immediately arranged for bail through the influence of a member of an outstanding law firm; a powerful friend telephoned a newspaper contact, and the report of the accident was not published. Within twenty-four hours, the girl was returned to school. In a few weeks the school authorities realized that the girl was pregnant and notified her parents. A psychiatrist was called in for consultation by the parents with the expectation, expressed frankly, that he was to recommend a therapeutic

§ August B. Hollingshead and Frederick C. Redlich, "Paths to the Psychiatrist," *Social Class and Mental Illness: A Community Study,* Wiley, New York, 1958, pp. 175–176.

interruption of the pregnancy. He did not see fit to do this and, instead, recommended hospitalization in a psychiatric institution to initiate psychotherapy. The parents, though disappointed that the girl would not have a "therapeutic" abortion, finally consented to hospitalization. In due course, the girl delivered a healthy baby who was placed for adoption. Throughout her stay in the hospital she received intensive psychotherapy and after being discharged continued in treatment with a highly regarded psychoanalyst.

The class V girl was arrested by the police after she was observed having intercourse with four or five sailors from a nearby naval base. At the end of a brief and perfunctory trial, the girl was sentenced to a reform school. After two years there she was paroled as an unpaid domestic. While on parole, she became involved in promiscuous activity, was caught by the police, and sent to the state reformatory for women. She accepted her sentence as deserved "punishment," but created enough disturbance in the reformatory to attract the attention of a guidance officer. This official recommended that a psychiatrist be consulted. The psychiatrist . . . was impressed by her crudeness and inability to communicate with him on most subjects. He was alienated by the fact that she thought masturbation was "bad," whereas intercourse with many men whom she hardly knew was "O.K." The psychiatrist's recommendation was to return the girl to her regular routine because she was not "able to profit from psychotherapy."

.   .   .

(26)

Family Planning and Poverty

FREDERICK S. JAFFE

The main finding of United States fertility studies during the last decade has been that many of the historic differentials are rapidly disappearing. Almost all Americans are coming to share a quite similar set of fertility values and practices. Some of the ancient differentials, such as those between urban and rural families, are narrowing considerably, and even the traditional inverse relationships between income (and related measures of socio-economic status) and family size have been reduced, and, for the most prosperous groups, even reversed.

Yet within this over-all and clear trend toward uniformity, there remain many paradoxes which demonstrate that control over fertility has not yet been realized universally in America. Despite the progress of the last 20 years, many low-income families, and a disproportionate number of nonwhite families, still remain very significantly outside the area of effective fertility control.

Among the factors which are responsible for this situation are the institutional and social mechanisms which are amenable to modification and correction by the serving professions. First, some data are presented which will help to establish the parameters of the problem.

§ Frederick S. Jaffe, "Family Planning and Poverty," reprinted from the *Journal of Marriage and the Family,* November 1964, pp. 467–470. By permission of publisher and author.

FAMILY SIZE PREFERENCES

A number of recent studies have shown, with remarkable consistency, that working-class Americans want as few children as, or fewer than, those of higher socio-economic status.

This is fully demonstrated in the 1960 Growth of American Families study, which is a replication of the 1955 GAF study of a representative national sample of white wives in their childbearing years. Nonwhite as well as white wives were sampled in 1960, thus providing the first overview of recent nonwhite fertility attitudes and practices.

The GAF investigators found that nine out of ten American wives, white and nonwhite, thought two to four children is the "ideal" size family, with the average minimum number 3.4 and the average maximum 3.5. In this study, "ideal" is a slightly different concept than "wanted." The number wanted at the time of the interview was smaller than the ideal: The average minimum number for all wives was 3.1, the average maximum 3.4. Lower-income couples wanted somewhat smaller families than higher-income couples. While the average maximum number of children wanted by husbands with family incomes of $10,000 or more was 3.3, the average maximum among those with incomes under $3,000 was 3.1.

It is especially noteworthy that nonwhites wanted a significantly smaller average number of children than whites. White wives wanted a minimum of 3.1 and a maximum of 3.5, while nonwhites wanted 2.7 and 3.0. Forty-six per cent of nonwhites wanted no more than two children, compared to 29 per cent of whites.

In a similar manner, the recent Princeton study showed that white collar wives wanted 3.3 children, compared to 3.2 for blue collar wives. And in a study by Bogue among Chicago families, the same preference of nonwhites for smaller families was shown. He found, for example, that 38 per cent of nonwhites regarded one or two children as ideal, compared to 21 per cent of whites.

There is some evidence that these findings apply also to the most impoverished Americans—those who are on relief and those who depend on public health facilities. The Greenleigh study of ADC families in Chicago reported that 90 per cent of mothers of out-of-wedlock children did not want to have the child. A 1963 paper from the Florida State Health Department showed that 70 per cent of more than 2,600 women attending maternity clinics wanted to have no more children. Two-thirds of this group were nonwhite, and they expressed a consistent desire to have fewer children than did white respondents.

Whether or not these findings can be regarded as definitive, they do tend to challenge some widely prevalent notions about lower-class fertility attitudes. Stycos has noted the remarkable similarity in many diverse societies of upper-class explanations for the high fertility of lower-class groups. The key proposition, he pointed out, is that ". . . the lower classes want many children . . . or do not care how many they have." The same explanation is commonly offered in this country—and it appears to bear approximately the same relationship to reality as most other middle-class explanations of lower-class behavior.

FERTILITY LEVELS

If lower-class attitudes favor small families, however, it is quite clear from census data and recent research that the wish is not quite the deed. In 1962, 34 per cent of the families with five children, and 44 per cent of those with six, had incomes below $4,000, compared to 20 per cent of the families with two children, and 22 per cent of those with three.

The 1960 GAF data show that one out of five couples with children have excess fertility, defined as those whose last child was unwanted by either husband or wife. Not surprisingly, the study found that ". . . the problem of unwanted pregnancies is most severe in the lower income and education groups." Among couples with excess fertility, it was found that those with lowest incomes expect more births than those with highest incomes . . . although those with lowest incomes want fewer. If the husband had an income of less than $3,000 and the last pregnancy was unwanted, the excess of births expected was 70 per cent. Only 11 per cent of the college-educated group fall into the excess fertility category, compared to 32 per cent of the grade school group. The authors conclude: . . . "Lower status couples don't have more children . . . simply because they want more. They have more children because some of them do not use contraception regularly and effectively. If the wife has a grade school education and if the husband has an income of less than $3,000 a year, then 39 per cent have excess fertility . . . the judgment that their fertility is too high is their own opinion."

CONTRACEPTIVE PRACTICES

Thus the fertility problems of impoverished Americans must be considered against the background of current family planning practices in the United States. Here the 1960 GAF findings are in the main familiar in that they reinforce and extend the results of the 1955 investigation.

In 1960, fertility control of some sort was favored by 96 per cent of Protestants, 98 per cent of Jews, and 85 per cent of Catholics. Among whites, 81 per cent had used *some* form of fertility control by 1960, six per cent expected to begin practicing it some time in the future, and ten per cent were subfertile. Thus almost everyone was practicing family planning after a fashion, although there still were some socioeconomic differentials—e.g., 93 per cent of college-educated wives had practiced fertility control or planned to, compared to 72 per cent of grade school wives.

Data on nonwhite practices and the breakdown of methods employed by different classes are not yet available. In the 1955 study, however, lower-status . . . wives more often utilized such relatively unreliable methods as douching . . .

and less often used such reliable methods as diaphragms
. . . than higher-status wives.

THE GAP BETWEEN ASPIRATION
AND PERFORMANCE

The gap between lower-class fertility aspirations and performance is usually explained by the fact that lower-class
couples do not use contraception as regularly as higher-class
couples, nor do they employ methods which are as effective.
This, in turn, has led to studies, most notably by Rainwater,
of what is generally termed the "motivation" problem. These
studies have been valuable in pointing up the partly different
cultural settings of lower-class families, not to speak of the
quite different living conditions. In so doing, they should
reinforce the need for more extensive and intensive services
to make fertility control a reality for low-income Americans.

Yet, by a curious inversion, these useful explorations have
been distorted by some public health and welfare officials
into a justification for failure to offer any contraceptive services to indigent families on the ground that "they won't use it
anyway." More generally, the motivational analysis has been
employed by some to obscure what would seem to be the first
order of business—the study of the concrete conditions under
which impoverished Americans receive their medical care,
and the bearing that these conditions and other institutional
factors may have on the availability of contraception to these
families.

For example, 82 per cent of married nonwhites in New
York City between 1955 and 1959 delivered their babies in
municipal hospitals or on ward services of voluntary hospitals, compared to 14.5 per cent of whites; in 1955, only
11.1 per cent of nonwhite mothers had a private physician in
attendance during delivery. In a Washington, D.C. study published in 1961, 75 per cent of nonwhite births were staff
cases. The 1961 report of the Obstetrical Statistical Coopera-
tive, based on 66,000 discharges at approximately 20 hos-

pitals in New York, New Haven, Hartford, Philadelphia, Denver, San Francisco, Baltimore, and Salt Lake City showed that nearly 94 per cent of nonwhite deliveries were on ward service, compared to 35 per cent of whites.

These figures make clear that the vast majority of non-white mothers do not have ready access to a private physician during the childbearing period. Most tax-supported hospitals still do not make contraceptive services routinely and easily available to their patients, and only the exceptional voluntary hospital operates a birth control clinic which ward patients can attend. Since the most effective methods of birth control are usually prescribed by private physicians for their private patients during the postpartum period, do not these related facts suggest a significant set of factors limiting the actual availability of effective fertility control measures for non-white families—and influencing their subsequent fertility performance? To what extent do similar considerations apply to impoverished whites?

Even before the advent of the oral birth control pills in 1960, contraception was acceptable to many low-income families. The 1960 GAF study, based still on conventional birth control methods, showed that the increase in contraceptive use over 1955 was greatest among couples in the lowest socio-economic group. The proportion of users of all forms of birth control among grade school graduates increased from 49 per cent in 1955 to 66 per cent in 1960.

It will be most interesting to see a study of the period after 1960, because there is considerable evidence that oral contraception has radically changed the picture. In Mecklenburg County, North Carolina, for example, the Health and Welfare Departments have been cooperating since 1960 in a joint project offering oral contraceptives free to a group consisting primarily of relief recipients. Of the 673 patients who en-rolled in the clinic, 75 per cent are still taking the pills regularly and effectively, and there have been no pregnancies in this group, although these patients previously had been quite prolific. Similar evidence of the acceptability of the oral pills among poor families comes from Bellevue Hospital in

New York, where an active clinic serving a relief and impoverished population was established in 1959, and where more than 90 per cent of the patients choose the orals. In Planned Parenthood clinics throughout the country, 70 per cent of the patients have incomes of under $4,000, and the pills have sparked a doubling of the patient load in the last five years. Between 1962 and 1963 alone, there was a 25 per cent increase in contraceptive patients and a 60 per cent increase in those on the pills.

This recent experience should prompt the development of a more precise concept of the elements that go into motivation for family planning—and particularly of the relationship between ease of access to competent instruction and the level of motivation required for successful practice. Do all Americans today have equal access to fertility control? Would it not be fruitful to study the access problem of impoverished Americans realistically, to examine critically the obstacles society places in the way of effective fertility control guidance and instruction for poor families—and then to remove these obstacles? For it is certainly still true that most public hospitals, health departments, and welfare agencies either do not provide contraceptive service at all—or compel a couple to run an obstacle course in order to secure what everyone else in the society regards virtually as part of the Bill of Rights. In this connection, the significance of the fact should be pondered that in many public hospitals, it is considerably easier for an impoverished mother to be sterilized than for her to receive instruction and supplies for contraception.

Among these obstacles are those who manage to transform what has become an everyday practice for most American families into a traumatic experience, such as the caseworker who told a Planned Parenthood field worker not long ago, quite seriously, that she "wouldn't dream of suggesting birth control to a client unless the client had been in deep therapy for at least two years." And, of course, there are the very physical arrangements of many public institutions, not to speak of the attitudinal problems of the serving professionals. How many middle-class couples would be practicing birth control effectively if it required first that the wife spend a half day in a dingy clinic waiting room, only to find that she has to defend her integrity against the indifference and hostility of a doctor who tells her that she ought to stop her sex life if she doesn't want children?

If that sounds extreme, it is useful to recall the story of Sadie Sachs which started Margaret Sanger on her work for birth control. As a public health nurse on New York's Lower East Side in 1912, Mrs. Sanger had carefully nursed back to life Mrs. Sachs, who was hemorrhaging after self-induced abortion. When Mrs. Sachs finally recovered, she asked the doctor to tell her how to keep from becoming pregnant. The doctor's immortal reply was: "Tell Jake to sleep on the roof."

A half century later, in 1962, CBS did a telecast on the birth control situation in Chicago. The program contained the following equally immortal words from a white Tennessee mother of six who had delivered her last baby at Cook County Hospital. Like Sadie Sachs, she had asked the doctor for birth control information. "Well," she told CBS, "I asked him what I could do and he said that was up to me to decide. He said one thing, that the best thing for me to do would not be close to my husband, and if I didn't want to get that way, it was up to me to stay away from getting pregnant until I had the operation coming up in April. Well, I didn't like it, 'cause I figure my husband's a human being just like he is, and I don't think he'd like to be told that—to stay away from his wife, if he's married."

SECTION VI

THE WAR
ON POVERTY

PRESIDENT JOHNSON, *following in the footsteps of his predecessor by making poverty one of his major concerns, created the slogan "The War on Poverty." In his message to Congress in March, 1964, he outlined the measures, embodied in the Economic Opportunity Act, which he considered essential to fight this war. The message is reprinted on page 202. The American optimistic belief that poverty can be completely obliterated in as rich a country as the United States, which also had been expressed in Roosevelt's inaugural address, and even Yates' report characterizes Johnson's message as well. The most important provisions of the Act are the Job Corps, the Work-Training and Work-Study Programs, and the training and utilization of a domestic volunteer corps, Volunteers in the Service of America (VISTA), to work in the slums and the areas of greatest deprivation. The Job Corps and the work-training programs will provide basic educational training and useful work experience for school dropouts and unemployed youth between 16 and 21, and the work-study programs will help high school and college students. While they are in a certain measure reminiscent of the CCC camps and the NYA of the depression period, the VISTA idea, a successor to President Kennedy's envisaged domestic peace corps, is a relatively new concept and, if carried out as conceived, may help the "two Americas" to understand each other somewhat better. "VISTA volunteers will bridge the widening gulf between the haves and the have nots in America. The poor cannot reach across this gulf." (From a pamphlet of the Office of Economic Opportunity [OEO].)*

Articles evaluating projects undertaken under the new programs are at the time of this writing not yet available. Suffice it to state that about 5 months after the passing of the Economic Opportunity Act (EOA) already 400 projects, partly ongoing and partly new, had been approved. They range from job corps in individual states, nationwide neighborhood youth corps for the establishment of summer jobs for high school students, general social action programs on a community wide basis for action and research, Operation Headstart providing pre-kindergarten training, to provision for VISTA workers on Indian reservations and loans to rural families.

There are, of course, any number of questions which arise in connection with such ambitious programs. The article by Alvin L. Schorr (page 210), raises some policy issues, especially the questions of opportunities and privileges. The very brief excerpt from an article in the New Republic *points up the difficulties in selection for job corps and other training possibilities, if one really wants to eliminate poverty (page 219).*

Another very vital aspect of the "war" is the question of how to reach the poor. We saw in Mary Wright's article (page 125) how confused a poor and uneducated man becomes when he is confronted with the complexities of modern bureaucratic organization. It is a well known fact to anyone familiar with the profession of social work in its modern form that the majority of the trained social caseworkers are psychoanalytically oriented and their agencies— privately supported family agencies and mental health clinics—serve, to the largest extent, middle class clients. The administration of the public assistance programs comprising among their clients about 20 percent of the poorest of the poor is left to untrained workers whose main function is the determination of eligibility requirements. Some new techniques in the case-work process have been tried on a small scale with so called multi-problem families. That the poor have little chance to receive modern psychiatric treatment was pointed out previously in Coles' article (page 181). Frank Riessman elaborates on a similar point in more detail: the treatment of the poor by social workers and clinical psychologists. He notes "involvement" of the poor as a possible new technique. Among others "Mobilization for Youth" on the lower East Side of New York has pioneered with this technique. MFY works as a kind of an intermediary between the individual and the existing bureaucratic organizations in a social action program. It also uses people from the district as case aides on a rather large scale. We see in Murray Kempton's article what happens, "When You Mobilize the Poor" (page 228). Finally we bring a case study, part of a larger project, which shows the different approaches used by health workers in two slum districts—the one effective, the other ineffective—and points out the general difficulties of middle class health agencies in reaching the poor.

Message to Congress (March 3, 1964) on Poverty

LYNDON B. JOHNSON

We are citizens of the richest and most fortunate nation in the history of the world.

One hundred and eighty years ago we were a small country struggling for survival on the margin of a hostile land.

Today we have established a civilization of free men which spans an entire continent.

With the growth of our country has come opportunity for our people—opportunity to educate our children, to use our energies in productive work, to increase our leisure—opportunity for almost every American to hope that through work and talent he could create a better life for himself and his family.

The path forward has not been an easy one.

But we have never lost sight of our goal: an America in which every citizen shares all the opportunities of his society, in which every man has a chance to advance his welfare to the limit of his capacities.

We have come a long way toward this goal.

We still have a long way to go.

The distance which remains is the measure of the great unfinished work of our society.

To finish that work I have called for a national *war on poverty*. Our objective: total victory.†

† The Economic Opportunity Act became Public Law 88–452 on August 20, 1964 with minor changes. Congress appropriated for the first year $784.2 millions. The Education Bill allotting $1.3 billion predominately for aid to public schools in areas of poverty was passed on April 9, 1965.

There are millions of Americans—one fifth of our people —who have not shared in the abundance which has been granted to most of us, and on whom the gates of opportunity have been closed.

What does this poverty mean to those who endure it?

It means a daily struggle to secure the necessities for even a meager existence. It means that the abundance, the comforts, the opportunities they see all around them are beyond their grasp.

Worst of all, it means hopelessness for the young.

The young man or woman who grows up without a decent education, in a broken home, in a hostile and squalid environment, in ill health or in the face of racial injustice—that young man or woman is often trapped in a life of poverty.

He does not have the skills demanded by a complex society. He does not know how to acquire those skills. He faces a mounting sense of despair which drains initiative and ambition and energy. . . .

The war on poverty is not a struggle simply to support people, to make them dependent on the generosity of others.

It is a struggle to give people a chance.

It is an effort to allow them to develop and use their capacities, as we have been allowed to develop and use ours, so that they can share, as others share, in the promise of this nation.

.   .   .

Our fight against poverty will be an investment in the most valuable of our resources—the skills and strength of our people.

And in the future, as in the past, this investment will return its cost many fold to our entire economy.

If we can raise the annual earnings of 10 million among the poor by only $1,000 we will have added 14 billion dollars a year to our national output. In addition we can make important reductions in public assistance payments which now cost us 4 billion dollars a year, and in the large costs of fighting crime and delinquency, disease and hunger.

This is only part of the story.

Our history has proved that each time we broaden the base of abundance, giving more people the chance to produce and consume, we create new industry, higher production, increased earnings and better income for all.

Giving new opportunity to those who have little will enrich the lives of all the rest.

Because it is right, because it is wise, and because, for the first time in our history, it is possible to conquer poverty, I submit, for the consideration of the Congress and the country, *the Economic Opportunity Act of 1964.*

The Act does not merely expand old programs or improve what is already being done.

It charts a new course.

It strikes at the causes, not just the consequences of poverty.

It can be a milestone in our one-hundred-eighty year search for a better life for our people.

This Act provides five basic opportunities.

It will give almost half a million underprivileged young Americans the opportunity to develop skills, continue education, and *find useful work.*

It will give every American community the opportunity to develop a *comprehensive plan to fight its own poverty*—and help them to carry out their plans.

It will give dedicated Americans the opportunity to enlist as *volunteers* in the war against poverty.

It will give many workers and farmers the opportunity to break through particular barriers which bar their escape from poverty.

It will give the entire nation the opportunity for a concerted attack on poverty through the establishment, under my direction, of the *Office of Economic Opportunity,* a national headquarters for the war against poverty.

This is how we propose to create these opportunities.

FIRST, we will give high priority to helping young Americans who lack skills, who have not completed their education or who cannot complete it because they are too poor.

The years of high school and college age are the most critical stage of a young person's life. If they are not helped then, many will be condemned to a life of poverty which they, in turn, will pass on to their children.

I therefore recommend the creation of a *Job Corps, a Work-Training Program,* and a *Work-Study Program.*

A new national Job Corps will build toward an enlistment of 100,000 young men. They will be drawn from those whose background, health and education make them least fit for useful work.

Those who volunteer will enter more than 100 Camps and Centers around the country.

Half of these young men will work, in the first year, on special conservation projects to give them education, useful work experience and to enrich the natural resources of the country.

Half of these young men will receive, in the first year, a blend of training, basic education and work experience in Job Training Centers.

These are not simply camps for the underprivileged. They are new educational institutions, comparable in innovation to the land grant colleges. Those who enter them will emerge better qualified to play a productive role in American society.

A new national Work-Training Program operated by the Department of Labor will provide work and training for 200,000 American men and women between the ages of 16 and 21. This will be developed through state and local governments and non-profit agencies.

Hundreds of thousands of young Americans badly need the experience, the income, and the sense of purpose which useful full- or part-time work can bring. For them such work may mean the difference between finishing school or dropping out. Vital community activities from hospitals and playgrounds to libraries and settlement houses are suffering because there are not enough people to staff them.

We are simply bringing these needs together.

A new national Work-Study Program operated by the Department of Health, Education, and Welfare will provide federal funds for part-time jobs for 140,000 young Americans who do not go to college because they cannot afford it.

There is no more senseless waste than the waste of the brainpower and skill of those who are kept from college by economic circumstance. Under this program they will, in a great American tradition, be able to work their way through school.

They and the country will be richer for it.

SECOND, through a new Community Action program we intend to strike at poverty at its source—in the streets of our cities and on the farms of our countryside among the very young and the impoverished old.

This program asks men and women throughout the country to prepare long-range plans for the attack on poverty in their own local communities.

These are not plans prepared in Washington and imposed upon hundreds of different situations.

They are based on the fact that local citizens best understand their own problems, and know best how to deal with those problems.

These plans will be local plans striking at the many unfilled needs which underlie poverty in each community, not just one or two. Their components and emphasis will differ as needs differ.

These plans will be local plans calling upon all the resources available to the community—federal and state, local and private, human and material.

And when these plans are approved by the Office of Economic Opportunity, the federal government will finance up to 90% of the additional cost for the first two years.

The most enduring strength of our nation is the huge reservoir of talent, initiative and leadership which exists at every level of our society.

Through the Community Action Program we call upon this, our greatest strength, to overcome our greatest weakness.

THIRD, I ask for the authority to *recruit and train skilled volunteers* for the war against poverty.

Thousands of Americans have volunteered to serve the needs of other lands.

Thousands more want the chance to serve the needs of their own land.

They should have that chance.

Among older people who have retired, as well as among the young, among women as well as men, there are many Americans who are ready to enlist in our war against poverty.

They have skills and dedication. They are badly needed.

If the State requests them, if the community needs and will use them, we will recruit and train them and give them the chance to serve.

FOURTH, we intend to create new opportunities for certain hard-hit groups to break out of the pattern of poverty.

Through a new program of loans and guarantees we can provide incentives to those who will employ the unemployed.

Through programs of work and retraining for unemployed fathers and mothers we can help them support their families in dignity while preparing themselves for new work.

Through funds to purchase needed land, organize cooperatives, and create new and adequate family farms we can help those whose life on the land has been a struggle without hope.

FIFTH, I do not intend that the war against poverty become a series of uncoordinated and unrelated efforts—that it perish for lack of leadership and direction.

Therefore this bill creates, in the Executive Office of the President, a new Office of Economic Opportunity. Its Director will be my personal Chief of Staff for the War against poverty. . . .

He will be directly responsible for these new programs. He will work with and through existing agencies of the government.

This program—the Economic Opportunity Act—is the foundation of our war against poverty. But it does not stand alone.

For the past three years this government has advanced a number of new proposals which strike at important areas of need and distress.

I ask the Congress to extend those which are already in action, and to establish those which have already been proposed.

There are programs to help badly distressed areas such as the Area Redevelopment Act, and the legislation now being prepared to help Appalachia.

There are programs to help those without training find a place in today's complex society—such as the Manpower Development Training Act and the Vocational Education Act for youth.

There are programs to protect those who are specially vulnerable to the ravages of poverty—hospital insurance for the elderly, protection of the migrant farm workers, a food stamp program for the needy, coverage for millions not now protected by a minimum wage, new and expanded unemployment benefits for men out of work, a Housing and Community Development bill for those seeking decent homes.

Finally there are programs which help the entire country, such as aid to education which, by raising the quality of schooling available to every American child, will give a new chance for knowledge to the children of the poor.

I ask immediate action on all these programs.

What you are being asked to consider is not a simple or an easy program. But poverty is not a simple or an easy enemy.

It cannot be driven from the land by a single attack on a single front. Were this so we would have conquered poverty long ago.

Nor can it be conquered by government alone.

For decades American labor and American business, private institutions and private individuals have been engaged in strengthening our economy and offering new opportunity to those in need.

We need their help, their support and their full participation.

Through this program we offer new incentives and new opportunities for cooperation, so that all the energy of our nation, not merely the efforts of government, can be brought to bear on our common enemy.

. . .

Today for the first time in our history, we have the power

to strike away the barriers to full participation in our society. Having the power, we have the duty.

The Congress is charged by the Constitution to "provide . . . for the general welfare of the United States." Our present abundance is a measure of its success in fulfilling that duty. Now Congress is being asked to extend that welfare to all our people.

. . .

The new program I propose is within our means. Its cost of 970 million dollars is 1% of our national budget—and every dollar I am requesting for this program is already included in the budget I sent to Congress in January.

But we cannot measure its importance by its cost.

For it charts an entirely new course of hope for our people.

We are fully aware that this program will not eliminate all the poverty in America in a few months or a few years. Poverty is deeply rooted and its causes are many.

But this program will show the way to new opportunities for millions of our fellow citizens.

It will provide a lever with which we can begin to open the door to our prosperity for those who have been kept outside.

It will also give us the chance to test our weapons, to try our energy and ideas and imagination for the many battles yet to come. As conditions change, and as experience illuminates our difficulties, we will be prepared to modify our strategy.

And this program is much more than a beginning.

Rather it is a commitment. It is a total commitment by this President and this Congress, and this nation, to pursue victory over the most ancient of mankind's enemies. . . .

On similar occasions in the past we have often been called upon to wage war against foreign enemies which threatened our freedom. Today we are asked to declare war on a domestic enemy which threatens the strength of our nation and the welfare of our people.

If we now move forward against this enemy—if we can bring to the challenges of peace the same determination and strength which has brought us victory in war—then this day and this Congress will have won a secure and honorable place in the history of the nation, and the enduring gratitude of generations of Americans yet to come.

⟦ 28 ⟧

Policy Issues in Fighting Poverty

ALVIN L. SCHORR

In our current approach to poor families in this country, those of us concerned with raising the levels of living are substantially embarked upon what might be called a case approach. We are untangling all the threads in the skein of poverty—attitude and environment, individual and family, motivation and opportunity. We muster this understanding in order to turn to the poor, family by family. We are aware that motivation, if it can be stimulated, must find a response in opportunity. But we are working, on the whole, from the family or individual outward. Only the painfully readjusting relationship of Negroes and whites represents a relevant fundamental change. This change, though significant, is not the only one that is required.

Since I am, by training and commitment, a social caseworker, I am convinced of the validity and importance of the case approach. Nevertheless, if we hope to make much progress with poor families, we must ask if the case approach is enough. Many kinds of ideas may be relevant in considering changes that would be desirable in the climate that surrounds

§ Alvin L. Schorr, "Policy Issues in Fighting Poverty," reprinted from *Children,* vol. 11, no. 4, pp. 227–131, Childrens Bureau, U.S. Department of Health, Education and Welfare, Washington, D.C.

poor people or in the structure of our society. To illustrate, I shall deal here with two kinds of ideas that seem profoundly important: the climate of social pressure in which we live and our view of equality.

In preparation for the 1960 White House Conference on Children and Youth, each State submitted a separate report. Curiously, despite some differences in facts reported from State to State, most State reports revealed a marked anxiety in appraising the trends. If an increasing number of women were working or if, on the other hand, women found it difficult to work, the consequence was in either case anxiety. Young people were marrying earlier; the damage that would result was described with alarm. Were the same young people failing to marry and, consequently, producing illegitimate children? States were certainly concerned about that. Moreover, one readily remembers when there was a trend toward *late* marriage—no doubt, a cause for alarm in the 1930's. These examples suggest that we tend to feel and operate under very great pressure.

A Tendency to Prescriptions

We tend increasingly, it appears, to address ourselves to one another in prescriptive terms. Do not smoke cigarettes! Do, even if you are a woman, be creative! . . .

These two points apply to all of us. How very natural, then, that the helping professions should bring pressure and prescriptiveness to bear upon the families who are our more or less voluntary clientele? Are we in fact exerting such pressure? The problem is recognizable at each of the levels at which we operate.

In face-to-face contact with families, there is a growing tendency to tell them what to do. The evidence that social workers are becoming increasingly prescriptive is assembled elsewhere. Educators are beginning to complain that the pressure in schools is bringing to college a "prematurely dry, harried, anxious undergraduate." Our hopeful recent invention, Peace Corpsmen, and other volunteers are least of all equipped to know the limitation of direct instruction. There is, of course, a wide range of situations in which simple instruction is appropriate. But there is also a wide range of situations in which prescriptions are inappropriate. Today the two kinds of situations are being confused.

Projects and People

When demonstration projects are being developed, insufficient thought is given to effects on people at the project's end. For example, we lavish equipment and staff upon kindergarten children, who then proceed into poverty-stricken first grades. We have learned how these children progress in their pre-school experimental phase, but what does the transition do—to personality as well as to learning? We have hundreds of counseling and training projects that sweep people up in a hopeful attempt to improve their circumstances. Many of these projects have a life of one year, during which we count up indications of their progress —training courses initiated, work undertaken, housekeeping improved. But what happens to these people when the project evaporates?

These questions do not simply ask whether conscientiously collected results are accurate. They make a more disturbing point. Projects that are brief or that are not fitted with the greatest care into people's lives may reinforce the most handicapping attitudes of poor people: Lucky today—unlucky tomorrow! It's no use trying because the cards are stacked! To the extent that casual projects even begin to succeed, the pressure of hope is added to the pressure from outside.

Finally, there is the public climate. As cut off as they may be, many poor people read newspapers and see television. The determination, which many of us share, to end poverty is reflected on millions of television screens in poor homes. Some families undoubtedly respond with pleasure. Others are fearful; they cannot be certain what is intended, and they feel the force of the determination being asserted. I happened to visit a high school the day after a metropolitan newspaper described its rehabilitative program. A social worker or public official might find the article admirable. The children saw it differently. They were angry at being called blighted and delinquent. They resented an apparent determination to change them. Nor was the faculty pleased. The newspaper's emphasis on the success of new staff members poked clumsily at a fragile sense of unity in staff relationships. . . .

We live, all of us, under pressure. In this circumstance, we may confuse war against poverty with pressure against poor people. These are not the same thing. On the contrary, it is self-volition that we hope to achieve. Self-volition is a hardier impulse than we sometimes recognize, but it is ironic to suppose that self-volition can be compelled. It would be pleasant to believe that this requires only a tactical change. Obviously, improved techniques and more thoughtfulness with client, project, and public pronouncement would help. But the fact that we need to be cautioned probably reflects a deeper problem. Pressure and prescriptiveness are rooted in our reactions to complexity and change and in our impatience at being thwarted. We may treat the poor worse than we treat one another; we shall hardly treat them better. . . .

Poverty and Alienation

We usually talk as if equality and opportunity were indistinguishable. Historically, equality of opportunity has been our major theme. But European travelers detected a separate theme and, in the nineteenth century, commented upon it with delight and awe. . . . In this definition of equality, a man is respected and respects himself no matter what his station or opportunity. But now we have a spate of descriptions that show that we are in rather a different situation. Many of us have been oblivious of poor people or viewed them, when necessary, with scorn. Very many of the poor, for their own part, view the rest of us with resentment or themselves with contempt. The technical term that sums up this development is "alienation."

It is an interesting fact that poverty in Europe does not appear to produce the same degree of alienation.

. . .

It has been observed before this that alienation need not accompany poverty. It seems necessary, therefore, to understand in what circumstances poor people feel and are accepted as integral to society. The explanations must include a closed class system, which we would reject, and a sense of working-class solidarity, which we have never achieved. The explanations must also include—and this is the point—that society will not move very far or fast without attempting, in some degree, to bring the poorest along. This is precisely where we have made our mistake since the war. *We have moved very far and very fast. We have not brought the poor along.* And we have the temerity to be surprised at their attitudes and, some of us, to proceed to study them as an alien social system.

Limitations of Opportunity

We are, of course, very seriously embarked on an effort to provide equality of opportunity. It is right to be pleased at this turn of events. But this effort can lead us to the beguiling misconception that equality of opportunity will narrow the gulf between privilege and poverty. The reasons that it will not narrow the gulf are already part of our knowledge.

First, opportunity is related to ability to seize opportunity. Understanding of this fact is the essence of our new sophistication but it presents a thorny problem. In France, for example, aid designed specifically for the poor goes disproportionately to those who need it less than others. In England, an avowed welfare state, housing for those in "housing need" benefits the poor less than others. In the United States too the poorest families tend not to get into public housing. They do not receive financial aids given for education. And we are discovering that those most in need of job training tend not to benefit from the program that Congress has enacted. If one steps back from the detailed problem in each particular program, one general point becomes clear. It is precisely characteristic of those who are poor that they cannot meet entrance requirements and cannot manipulate bureaucracies. On the other hand, those who are not poor are resourceful in these matters. We have so far dealt with this problem by devising better rules from time to time. This misses the heart of the problem: the poorest are the least able to use any rules.

Privileges Beyond Income

Second, in the United States privilege can no longer be audited in dollar income. To know privilege, one must count tax advantages and chargeable business costs, the favors of one's debtors and wooers, and conventions and sabbaticals.

One must count also the distribution of public services. It is generally assumed that public services tend to benefit those who are poor; but it would be useful to perform a balancing-up. Education is the largest expense of local governments. It is a familiar, if uncomfortable, fact that those who are poor get the worst public schools. To take another example, the roads and highways are public but mass transit is largely private. Public roads benefit those who have cars, while the poor pay their way. In short, in the years to come a major share of advancement in standards of living may occur in forms that do not show up in average family income. . . .

These first two points test the limits of what we mean by equality of opportunity. If we are talking of nineteenth century opportunity—that is, formal opportunities for cash income—we shall still be left with serious twentieth century inequity. In any case, the final point reaches deeper. In the end, opportunity means jobs, but many are poor who are not available to work. Many are poor because they are old. Are we taking a long view? There are people who will be poor 50 years from now because they have not had adequate homes and schooling in the past 15 years.

Many children are poor because they are socially orphaned.

They are born into families in which, although a father has not died, there is no genuine father. For the mothers in many of these families, work cannot be a solution. Work may be an ultimate solution for the children, but are they to be poor meanwhile?

Other people cannot use opportunity because, in one way or another, they are disabled; because they cannot learn a new skill at the time they must; because the effort on which we are embarked will, at its best, fail to reach everyone.

Finally, we must recognize that we are no longer in a situation in which there is likely to be work for *comparatively* unskilled people. We have not yet arranged to provide the number of jobs that will be wanted. On the contrary, in the net we are losing jobs every week. Until we see our way clear to rectifying this, we should not have unreal expectations from occupational training. By the most extravagant estimate, perhaps no more than half the poor families could reasonably improve their situations if suitable training were provided and a connection with a job arranged.

A Commitment to Oneness

For these reasons, opportunity will not unaided produce respect for man, as man. The three D's of alienation—drugs, delinquency, and despair—are already rife. We face the prospect that the gulf between the prosperous and the poor will widen. The statistics of poverty will count fewer of the untrained, but the remainder will be familiar—the aged, the families headed by women, the less well (though better than now) educated. These will be the new (or still) alienated class—smaller, perhaps, but ever more cut off.

We shall pursue the business of being one Nation, or we shall be divided. The objective of achieving an integrated society is equivalent in importance to that of wiping out poverty. It requires measures of its own. What might they be?

The present attack on poverty moves in the right direction. It sets out to commit the Nation to oneness. But clearly we are required to make this commitment on a new scale. One opportunity for such a commitment lies in our ability to produce goods at a continually increasing rate. We might, then, declare a moratorium on self-aggrandizement among the prosperous. That is, for the next 10 years we might undertake to invest the *annual increase* in Gross National Product in our own poor people and, although this is another question, in the poor people of the world.

In the first year this would amount to $20 billion, perhaps more—assuming a net increase of GNP over population. Does the figure seem fanciful? If we provided public assistance for children at the less than adequate level at which we now provide it for old people, we should be spending $4.5 billion more on public assistance alone. And we must think of much more than public assistance—education, medical care, housing, job training, social security, and so forth. A moratorium would move us to think in the magnitudes that are required to abolish poverty, but it would do more. All of us would be investing potential goods in the effort rather than only sentiment. More important, a moratorium would give us a symbol for what has not so far been brought into focus—an integrated society.

It does not seem appropriate to attempt to spell out the mechanics of a moratorium. A few observations may be necessary, however, to avoid an appearance of naivete. A moratorium need not interfere with self-advancement. It does not refer to normal profits and salary raises, but to the additional 3 or 4 percent of goods and services that our economy can produce each year. Nor does it refer to goods that must be allocated to actual population growth. A moratorium would probably require no management devices that we do not already extensively use—that is, control of taxes, money, and credit.

We might, in the end, be giving up very little: It may be a necessary condition of long-range advance that the poorest be given a radical step toward adequacy. This point has been made by Gunnar Myrdal. Furthermore, I am convinced that to those of us who have a decent income the continually rising standard of living brings no satisfaction. We should be relieved and delighted to substitute for a new refrigerator or a second television set, a sense of commitment and community.

Organization of the Disadvantaged

Let us turn to a second measure or series of measures that may assist in achieving an integrated society—more aid and encouragement to poor families to organize for their own purposes. Here, at any rate, we have an objective to which we have given lip-service. Some work runs aground on middle-class assumptions and language. Social agencies are now keenly aware of this problem. Some work runs aground because those who attempt it have ulterior motives. They seek citizen participation in an area that is to be cleared for urban renewal. Often poor people suspect—out of prior experience—that they are only to be used for someone else's purposes. The suspicion may preclude communication even when it is mistaken.

But there is the beginning of other work that is more successful. Civil rights groups such as CORE and SNCC started to move forward when, turning their backs on charitable objectives, they began to operate out of self-respect and self-interest. Therefore they have paid rather little attention to public asistance recipients and public housing residents. Now, however, on the East coast at least, demonstrations for more liberal assistance and better housing have been organized among the poorest Negro groups.

The best of the organized community efforts to deal with juvenile delinquency also attempt to assist poor people in organizing for their own ends. To be sure, Mobilization for Youth has a more difficult problem than CORE. Though conscious that hidden motives can destroy its usefulness to poor people, MFY must nevertheless keep minimal peace with the Establishment. Even the attempt is hopeful, but a sound resolution of this problem has yet to be worked out.

The problem of self-organization among poor white people is, in a way, more acute than among poor Negroes. Poor white people have no comparable movement and they are losing even the advantage that a white skin gave. If they are not reached in some other manner first, they may be candidates for a *White* Muslim movement.

At the core of the problem of stimulating self-organization is the anxiety that it provokes in many of us. Where militant organization takes place, it proves profoundly unsettling to the administrators who are involved. One may wonder where self-organization will end, once it begins. Research in the civil rights movement teaches something about this. It has been observed that the crime rate among Negroes drops sharply where protest action begins. The moral is clear. We have not a choice between tension and peace. We have a choice between tension that is constructive and tension that is destructive. . . .

〖 29 〗

Job Corps—What Boys Will it Take?

PATRICK ANDERSON

. . . Dr. Charles W. Slack, a training consultant for the Westinghouse Corporation, said in a recent memo circulated among the poverty staff:

"When I visit Washington these days, I hear much talk about selection procedures and other means for eliminating the undeserving poor from the Job Corps camps and centers, and from community action programs. The undeserving poor include the psychotic, the criminally inclined and perverted. Lately I notice that the 'undeserving poor' also seem to in-

§ Patrick Anderson, "Job Corps—What Boys Will It Take?" reprinted from *The New Republic*, February 20, 1965, p. 16.

clude the recalcitrant and difficult to handle, those who cannot adjust to institutional life, the overly aggressive, the
physically ill, and 'those who simply cannot adjust to group
participation' . . . the poverty program is for the deserving
poor, not the undeserving poor . . . if the poverty program
had been initiated with the idea of providing help for those
who deserved it and needed it, one would have no complaint
with the present trend away from the undeserving poor, but
in fact the poverty program was started with the intention
of eliminating poverty and the effects of poverty. It is conceivable that the program as it is now operating will do the
opposite. . . ."

⟮ 30 ⟯

New Models for Treatment of
Low Income Groups

FRANK RIESSMAN

As presently organized, treatment for mental and emotional problems is tacitly aimed at middle-class people. They
are preferred as clients, are considered more congenial, more
tractable, and better prospects for success. It is easier to talk
to them. Treatment, however, does not fit the attitudes and
life styles of the poor and is often not understood by them. In
essence, the poor are alienated from the very psychiatric and
psychological help they may need.

Increasing evidence demonstrates that the traditional tests,

§ Frank Riessman, "New Models for Treatment of Low Income
Groups," reprinted from *Trans-Action*, vol. 1, January 1964, pp. 8-11,
The Community Leadership Project, Washington University.

and the testing situation itself, are simply not designed for poor people. Testing and interviews are somber, formal and confining experiences. They are unfamiliar and unsettling to the low income individual. Not all of what we call "treatment" is scientific: there are cultural and value elements built into it as well. The office setting, dress, modes of speech, emphasis on planning for the future, and on "talking," almost always emphasize middle-class standards.

In a recent study William Haase found that essentially identical Rorschach ink-blot test records were interpreted differently depending on the social class of the patient. The low-income patients were more often classified as psychotic or having serious character disorders, while their middle-class equivalents were merely labeled neurotic, or dismissed as normal. Haase points out that since the poor have less opportunity and greater hardships than the middle-class, similar test records may indicate greater, not lesser, mental health. These are not isolated findings.

A common view is that mental treatment does not work well with the poor because, among other things, they are not introspective and desire specific directions. But the poor have certain assets for treatment that the middle-class do not have—they do not intellectualize or hide their feelings nearly so much, for one thing—and these strengths can be used successfully.

. . .

The remarks that follow attempt to sketch out several strategies for working with low-income clients which, if not new, are still unfamiliar to many.

Pre-Training

A two-fold strategy is needed (1) to modify the treatment (particularly the value elements or extra-scientific parts) to accommodate the low-income client; and (2) to educate and prepare him for those necessary parts of treatment with which he is unfamiliar.

Pre-training of the low-income client should prepare him:

To express personal feelings to a professional other than a
minister or priest;

To expect no miracles and understand that personality change
takes time;

To recognize that talk can be useful;

To understand that change requires work that he must do
himself;

To accept the knowledge that some of his difficulties are self-
inflicted, through inadequate thinking and defensive attitudes;

To understand that some physical problems and ailments can
be, in part at least, caused by psychological stresses;

To realize that one can criticize his family and still love and
respect it.

Preliminary consultations should be cut short and treatment begun as soon as possible. Dramatic and pictorial techniques, home interviews, and more informal methods should
be used, and a greater effort made to understand the patient
on his own terms. With the start of the treatment itself, the
usual routines should be changed to bring about quicker and
fuller understanding between therapist and client.

Instead of detailed questions about the patient's background,
and long explanations of the function and operation of the
agency, the therapist might simply encourage the patient to
talk and express his feelings, however subjectively, and
without worrying about complete accuracy of detail. This
may not only supply much information, but can give the
client release by "getting it off his chest."

Whatever minimum specific information needs to be recorded can be put off till the next meeting.

Where relevant and possible the therapist might talk about
himself, making common cause ("I had a problem like that
once." "I come from a neighborhood like yours.")

John P. Spiegel has found that promising results can be
achieved by relaxing the traditional treatment ideas of remaining nonresponsive and "neutral." Therapists can do this

by stating their personal ideas and feelings more frankly, by answering personal questions about themselves, by admitting when they find themselves ashamed of feelings that make their patients ashamed.

The therapist can indicate that paper work is as unpleasant to him as to the client, that he too disapproves of red-tape. . . .

The low-income client can accept authority when it is combined with informal friendliness.

Stage one then, beginning with the first interview and continuing through the first four or five meetings, should provide help, immediate service and advice, and give the patient a chance to unburden himself in an informal atmosphere where he feels he will be understood or at least accepted.

Acting Out: Role Playing

Another very different and promising approach to low-income patients might be explored—that of acting out situations, not on the usual group basis, but directly between the *worker* and the *patient*. Parent-child problems and marital and job difficulties might be handled this way, especially with young men who are opposed to "just talk." This approach has many advantages:

The therapist can immediately and dramatically reduce the distance between himself and the patient;

The emotions stirred up and revealed by role playing can induce better insight by the patient into his difficulties as well as better carry-through.

The patient's resentment and hostility toward the therapist can be expressed and handled more easily in role play than in direct confrontation.

The "Skilled Amateur"

In recent years there has been an increasing trend toward using nonprofessionals or skilled amateurs in work with low-income people. The professionals, with middle-class backgrounds and college training, find it much more difficult to make contact with the poor than do indigenous nonprofessionals.

Many of these amateurs are very talented in working with low-income people. However, as Herbert J. Gans points out, since they do not always recognize their own talent or know that it is of any use, they are not always easy to find. The function they serve—mediation between the classes—is a very useful one, and they are now being used as workers with delinquents, in interviewing, and as parent education aides in schools.

While they work superbly in some jobs, and in establishing communication across class lines, they are short on expertise. It is important therefore that they be supervised and trained by professionals.

The Candid Approach

There are a number of reasons why an approach that strongly emphasizes candor at every possible point may be especially important to the low income client. The poor know that they have been manipulated by so many agencies and institutions in our society—politicians, newspapers, social agencies—that they are often suspicious and bitter.

What is the "candid" approach? Isn't all treatment honest? As a matter of fact, no—most treatment cannot be honest all the time. But honesty can be stressed, and can be chosen when there is a choice.

There are at least two fundamental reasons why fully candid treatment is not always possible:

The client may not, at the beginning, be able to bear complete honesty.

Tactically, in some situations, it may be necessary not to reveal the whole truth right away. A worker with street gangs, for example, while being as honest as he can, cannot always tell all his intentions in the early stages of establishing contact.

Sometimes, however, therapists have carried this evasion too far. One of the disturbing effects of using "only a little" cheating and manipulation is that, eventually, it may begin to have meaning for its own sake—the worker becomes heavily involved in "out-cunning" the "manipulators" and comes to enjoy the game. He may use the manipulation to build himself up at the expense of the youths he is supposed to be helping.

The essential characteristics of a candid approach include:

The treatment agent (caseworker, detached worker, or whoever) does not pretend by his clothes, language or manner to "be one of the boys."

He does not lie to or manipulate the client about either small or large things.

He directly exposes the manipulation and maneuvering of the individual or group with which he is working. Criticism is open, direct and above-board; self-deception is exposed.

The real consequences of such things as drug addiction and alcoholism are carefuly and truthfully detailed.

The honest treatment agent is genuinely concerned but is not indulgent. He does not pretend to be a "buddy" and his criticism is open.

He makes clear that the change in behavior sought is not desired because it pleases him personally or the group, and that it will not be rewarded in those terms.

Generally, the candid approach is designed to discourage props and crutches. It demands effort, initiative, and responsibility from the patient. In treating a drug addict, for example, the aim is to get him out of institutions and face the responsibility of living in the community.

The candid approach, however, must be distinguished from the "hard line." Honesty is not punitive, authoritarian or moralizing. It is not self-righteous. Its aim is not conformity. To point out the consequences of behavior does not mean preaching "right" behavior. However it is obvious that such responses as violence or drug addiction, apart from any other implications, are neither practical nor profitable ways of changing reality, and this can be strongly emphasized.

Mobilization for Youth

Low-income people are subjected to many pressures that they do not have the skill, training and resources to handle. This results in despair, anxiety, and apathy and accounts for many of the mental and emotional difficulties of low-income groups.

The approach of certain community action programs, such as Mobilization for Youth in New York, is to act as a bridge between low-income groups and the community resources which are available, to provide support and help, and to reduce pressures to a point where they can be managed. The Mobilization for Youth program stresses the following:

Providing *information* about a wide range of community resources—including the school system and public transportation;

Teaching *skills* such as budgeting, home management, and child care;

Acting as *intermediaries* in dealings with governmental and other bureaucracies, in which the poor tend to feel especially inadequate;

Offering the *direct services* of nurses, baby sitters, homemakers and escorts to ease the daily burdens of low-income living, and to allow available vocational, medical, and other community services to be used more fully;

Offering *immediate help* in time of trouble or emotional distress—"emergency psychological first aid."

Involvement

Offering concrete service and information is very important. All of the techniques for establishing sympathy and trust are quickly dissipated if real service is not soon forthcoming. The poor are pragmatic; the low income client knows or quickly learns whether anyone really wants to or can help him, and if not, he is soon alienated, despite any amount of "sympathy" or "rapport."

The poor person, like everyone else, is involved in mankind. His problems and difficulties are not peculiar to him; they are shared by others who may organize to do something about them. He often feels alienated, helpless, and alone. We often find, however, that his psychological difficulties diminish in importance when he becomes involved in some larger commitment, activity, or social movement. This commitment can be to religion, a community organization, a labor union, a political movement, or even a hobby.

Many of the poor and disadvantaged are colored. Most therefore have a great interest, either open or latent, in today's movements toward equal opportunities and civil rights. Therapists, accustomed to the usual clinical approach, tend to underestimate the treatment value of such involvement. I oppose pressuring Negro clients to become interested in the Negro movement; but therapists should be alert to the possibilities it offers for mental health when such interest already exists.

Drug Addict Needs Faith

It is well to remember the apparent success of the Black Muslim movement in curtailing drug addiction and alcoholism among its members. This is particularly impressive in view of the generally acknowledged failure of the standard treatments for drug addiction; this is probably connected with the ideological and emotional appeal of the movement, whatever we may think of its racist aspects. Kenneth Marshall points up the issue by noting that the social worker who tries to change the drug addict "without offering him a faith in addition" has a much harder task than does the Muslim movement.

Social involvement may be very useful in treatment for two reasons:

Involvement provides a source of strength independent of the treatment agent. Any tendency the client may have to use the agent, and treatment itself, as crutches can be avoided.

The patient comes to identify with something larger than himself, becomes a part of it, and this may lead him to feel a growing sense of power, conviction and self-confidence that can affect all his relationships for the better. These, in turn, by making the circumstances of his life happier, can bring about further improvement.

Unquestionably there are some dangers in this involvement approach—as in any new technique for making treatment more readily available for the poor. But perhaps it is time to move out—and if need be to err—in new directions.

⟨ 31 ⟩

When You Mobilize the Poor

MURRAY KEMPTON

. . . The federal government had granted "Mobilization for Youth" $8 million, New York City $3 million and Ford Foundation $2 million for a three-year effort to discover how much of the blight of urban poverty might be erased by the efforts of the poor themselves.

Three-fifths of this $13 million went into job training and work projects for the unemployed young and into special efforts to improve an education system which leaves some 60 percent of the lower East Side's Puerto Rican school children three years behind the normal reading level by the time they reach the eighth grade. But these were orthodox remedies.

§ Murray Kempton, "When You Mobilize the Poor," reprinted from *The New Republic*, December 5, 1964, pp. 11–13 (copyright © 1964, Harrison-Blaine of New Jersey, Inc.), by permission.

. . . Mobilization has devoted the rest of its budget to a variety of other services, among them a staff of lawyers for welfare clients; a housing unit which keeps a register of those landlords who offend most against the comfort of their tenants; and a group of organizers whose duty it is to advise and assist lower East Siders in joining to change their lives by using the power the poor have rarely known they had. Mobilization quite badly describes the object of this last, its community action program, as "to teach the means of social protest." . . .

Teaching social protest is most of what is new about Mobilization for Youth. It also, among more tangible things, teaches the unemployed drop out how to dress when he applies for a job. That is useful knowledge, and so is the training in gas station service at the model garage donated by the Shell Oil Company, and the sewing classes with equipment donated by the International Ladies Garment Workers Union. But these are old-fashioned ways of improving the poor. . . .

Mobilization can be proud, of course, that 119 of its 157 on-the-job trainees had found places in private industry last July. But everything that is tangible is on this small a scale and in continual conflict with reality. Mobilization had thought, for example, of using the unemployed to repair dilapidated buildings; but if they do their landlords could, under the law, raise the rent $20 a month—"a hardship for some tenants." Mobilization can also work through ordinary channels of civic redress: its housing-service unit processes complaints to the building department. . . . Still, the results of adherence to ordinary city procedures do not encourage much: "the average wait for cases examined by the building department was almost five months—almost 90 percent of the leaky and unplastered ceilings and walls and floors remained unrepaired."

The $1,260,000 Mobilization allots the Board of Education for special services for schools cannot really be measured for results. Devoted as they are, the lower East Side's teachers suffer from an environmental gap between themselves and their Spanish pupils. One Mobilization project pays a teacher $11.50 for a two-hour visit to any pupil's home. The offer has drawn disappointingly few acceptances. "A number of teachers said they were afraid to go into these houses," one Mobilization professional reported. "That seemed to us sad, because welfare workers go there all the time and never worry."

The conventional devices of social adjustment have had results scanty enough, then, to reinforce the original interest of Mobilization's staff members in social protest. The main hope of Mobilization's more intense staff members is . . . to "organize the unaffiliated—to overturn the status quo and replace it with a higher level of stability, without delinquents, alcoholism or drug addiction."

The community action program which is their main instrument for teaching protest has changed the lower East Side hardly at all, yet the little it has done has affronted almost every city agency, from the police to the Department of Public Welfare. . . . In the past year Mobilization for Youth has given advice and financial assistance to the Council of Puerto Rican Organizations, which has a committee on police brutality; it has organized a Negro action group, of whose status as "the focal point of the Negro revolution" it is proud; it has helped develop the lower East Side rent strike. It is, then, at war with what is established, which means that it is inevitably at war with city agencies and the courts. Its program helps the citizen by harassing his local government. . . .

Mobilization's first troubles came in August, 1963, when a group of its workers mustered a lower East Side delegation to the March on Washington. Because Mobilization is supported by federal funds, the FBI conducted an investigation of their part in a ceremony to which President Kennedy had been invited. The Bureau checked the roster of Mobilization's 300 staff members and seems to have determined that 32 percent of them had once had connections with organizations on its subversive list.

. . . A source of continual annoyance to the Police Department was the increased public demand for an independent civilian board to review complaints of excessive force by policemen, which Mobilization's directors supported with a resolution.

A few weeks later, the *New York Daily News* published the first of a series of exposures of Mobilization for Youth as a focus of subversion. . . .

Mobilization itself struggles to investigate the charges against its staff workers and to make a dignified peace with official New York.

. . . The Director of Mobilization's legal service unit's . . . prime function is as a lawyer for persons on public relief, and we have been raised to believe that an object of charity does not argue with the society which dispenses it. The New York welfare system is by now so refined that it allots 48 bobby pins a year to every unemployed woman, and nine haircuts to every unemployed man. There is no such precision in the definition of the rights of its clients; they are ruled by the discretion of welfare workers who, in the best of cases, are under continual reminders to keep costs down. . . .

New York has long been afflicted with public complaints of vast immigrations of the indigent for no purpose except to get on relief. In 1961, its legislature finally passed a "Welfare Abuses" Act which would deny benefits to any person who came to New York with the primary purpose of getting on public assistance. . . . In the Act's first 10 months, 2,730 migrants were denied relief on the findings that they had come here looking for it. The burden of proof was on them.

Last year, S. took the case of a Puerto Rican family which had been refused assistance under the Welfare Abuse Law and won it before the State Board of Social Welfare. He says that he believes that as many as 2,700 of the first 2,730 ineligibles would also have won their cases if there had been lawyers to help them.

. . . Until now there has been almost no litigation to raise public welfare to the level Katzenbach (the Attorney General) describes as justice rather than charity. There is, for example, a serious question whether welfare residence laws are constitutional, but no lawyer has ever brought a case. We are a society where rights are defined by adversary proceedings in court. The welfare client, having not before had many lawyers, has not until now had rights. His appearance with counsel is not a prospect to make the best Welfare Commissioner happy; . . .

A further inconvenience attendant upon Mobilization's attitude toward the poor is demonstrated by its policy of seeking residents of the neighborhood and employing them as community workers. It has so far hired 40 of this class it calls "the low-paid nonprofessional worker."

. . . Mobilization for Youth has taken the risk of treating the poor as factors in their own destiny. How high a risk that was we can see from Mobilization's present troubles.

The federal and city governments and a great private foundation joined in Mobilization's huge grant because they wanted an experiment in engaging and changing the social pattern of poverty. The lesson, we must assume, would be learned not from old ways Mobilization used, whose results were worthy but modest, but from the new ones whose results were disturbance and are now hostility from every instrument of organized local society.

〖 32 〗

Reaching the Tuberculous Poor

JERE A. WYSONG AND ROBERT L. EICHHORN

Middle-class health organizations have proved themselves least effective in those parts of the city and among those

§Jere Wysong and Robert Eichhorn, Sociology Department, Purdue University. Original contribution to this publication.

groups where tuberculosis is at its worst. The disease is most prevalent among the urban poor, the derelicts of Skid Row, Negroes, and the newly arrived from Puerto Rico or Appalachia. . . . The few blocks that make up Skid Row in Chicago contribute about one-fifth of the city's cases, and Negroes are three times more likely to develop tuberculosis than whites. A tuberculosis screening program in Chicago may yield one suspect from every 50 X-rays taken in the poorer sections compared to one in every 500 in white-collar neighborhoods.

HEALTH AGENCIES, EXCHANGE AND THE CULTURE OF POVERTY

Tuberculosis control demands a degree of coordination among public and private agencies and a sensitivity to the cultural milieu in which they are working that are characteristically lacking. Many of the difficulties in finding and treating the tubercular are rooted in the organization of medical care. Many other difficulties are due to the inability of middle-class health organizations to adapt tuberculosis control programs to the culture of poverty.

The sheer number of organizations concerned with the disease operates against an orderly progression through the treatment process. In Cook County, for instance, tuberculosis control is of interest to federal, state, county, and city officials as well as representatives of the voluntary health associations and other citizen groups. There are city and county sanatoriums, out-patient clinics, several city health departments, local medical associations, hospitals, nursing homes, welfare agencies, public housing authorities, school systems, police departments, jails, courts, political parties, churches, urban renewal programs, industrial health clinics, ethnic organizations and tax payers associations.

The network of relationships among these organizations is exceedingly complex, reflecting differences in goals, size, structure, skills and ideologies. . . . Welfare agencies are likely to be involved in tuberculosis control because the patient's family has become dependent; public health officers receive reports from doctors and refer patients to sanatoriums or clinics; public health nurses cooperate with sanatoriums in checking the contacts of tuberculars; courts may be called upon to judge whether a patient shall be forcibly hospitalized; hospitals and schools are often asked to aid in case detection programs; police may refer cases to sanatoriums; and the voluntary tuberculosis associations often carry on programs of public education and case detection through the schools, churches, industries and service organizations. Control of a disease that requires early diagnosis, intensive treatment and prolonged surveillance is made difficult by an organizational arrangement such as this. Yet some agencies devoted to tuberculosis control are more effective in reaching the poor than others. Successful organizations, we submit, understand and adapt their programs to the culture of poverty: they establish meaningful *exchange* relations with the poor.

According to sociologist George Homans, relations between an organization and its clientele can be viewed as an exchange of goods and service, tangible or intangible, and more or less rewarding or costly. A tuberculosis association provides free chest X-rays for its clients, who in turn through their cooperation furnish the association with its reason for existence. An agency that provides benefits for a client obligates him. Failure to reciprocate means that the relation will be severed. Exchange, as the word implies, is a two-way process, and for it to work *each party in the transaction must offer something of value to the other.* Herein lies the key to the failure of many health agencies to reach the tuberculous poor.

Health agencies directly concerned with tuberculosis control subscribe to a set of values, derived in large measure from the medical system of which they are a part. Agency personnel assume that (1) life is worth saving, (2) tuberculosis is a serious threat to health and life, (3) life can be preserved through reliance upon medical science and technology, and (4) denying oneself the pleasure of the moment for some greater gain in the future, such as good health, is only common sense. Programs for reaching the tuberculous poor are designed in harmony with these values. Handbills describe the symptoms of the disease, assuming that only lack of information prevents people from entering the treatment cycle. The tubercular who eludes health educator and police alike is an enigma. Yet within his own scheme of values, within the culture of poverty, the behavior of the tubercular is eminently sensible. The obligation to provide for his family may loom more important than the preservation of life. Tuberculosis may seem minor compared to drug addiction. Doctors may frighten rather than reassure. And months in the sanatorium may seem too great a price to pay for recovery.

The health agency that is able to recognize its own value premises and translate them into terms that have meaning for the poor, bridging the gap between the two cultures, will be more successful in tuberculosis control. This agency will make available to the poor the achievements of present day medical science.

There follows a description and evaluation of one voluntary agency's attempt to X-ray the urban poor in two high-incidence areas of Chicago. In a Negro residential neighborhood, the agency's professional health educators approached the poor through local organizations. On Skid Row, the health educator contacted the men on the street. In the latter instance, the agency had something to exchange for cooperation: in the former, it had nothing to give.

HEALTH EDUCATORS BEHIND THE GOLD COAST: A FAILURE

The target for two health educators was a population of 40,000 poor, living in a neighborhood of converted hotels, deteriorated brownstones, frame tenements, and high-rise public housing on Chicago's North side. The Negro majority, the Puerto Ricans and Mexicans, and the remnants of the

Irish and Italian groups that preceded them are strangers to the businessman of the downtown area to the south, the social elite in the plush apartment buildings to the east, and the executives of the commercial and industrial firms that bound the community on the west. These ethnic groups are also, in some senses, strangers to each other: the indigenous organizations that have emerged to meet the problems of the community often reflect the conflicts between groups in their goals and memberships. For the most part, however, the local clubs and societies are concerned with problems common to the entire neighborhood, and conflict is not severe.

The problems of the area are typical of transitional zones. Overcrowded, deteriorated tenements owned by absentee landlords and inadequate sanitation and garbage collection are painfully obvious to neighborhood leaders. Unemployment is common, while welfare dependency is a way of life. Both are perpetuated by inadequate educational facilities. Crimes committed in the neighborhood include assaults in the stair-wells of the housing projects, gang delinquency, and organized gambling and prostitution. These almost obscure the problem of tuberculosis in the neighborhood. Few residents or community leaders know how widespread tuberculosis is among them. In 1961, there were over 140 new active cases reported for the area and 22 deaths. A tuberculin testing program in public and parochial schools showed that 28% of the older children were already infected.

The two health educators, armed with speeches and statistics on tuberculosis, tried throughout one entire summer to persuade the residents of the neighborhood to go through the X-ray unit, the first step in the treatment cycle. They gave talks at community centers and recruited volunteers from building committees and the churches. The mobile X-ray unit visited 55 locations in the neighborhood in over 80 full days of operation. The entire program was meant to be a community-wide campaign against tuberculosis. *But the campaign never really began.* The meetings sponsored by the housing authority were poorly attended, the building committee presidents and local leaders did not get "their people" out for the X-ray, and the few volunteers recruited to help at the X-ray unit did not appear. The X-ray technicians and health educators spent the summer at the units waiting for people who did not come. At summer's end only 9,500 residents had been through the X-ray unit, yielding 150 suspects.

The campaign failed because the health educators approached this slum community as they would suburban Glencoe or Park Forest. On the outskirts of the city one could assume consensus about the importance of health, the efficacy of an appeal to reason, the presence of organizations that would mobilize community support for tuberculosis control, and immunity from involvement in divisive issues that would compromise or embarrass the agency. X-rays were exchanged for the satisfaction of participating in a worthy cause and for confirmation of what the suburbanite already knew, that he was free of tuberculosis. But free X-rays were not attractive to the Negro who wanted to avoid contact with white outsiders or the middle-aged man who was ashamed to admit he could not write his own name on the X-ray card. Many feared being "caught," separated from their family, and confined in a sanatorium. Others were intimidated by the shiny truck and its complex machinery. And the health educators' appeals, couched in terms of good health, a brighter future and confidence in medical science fell on deaf ears. Since the cost of an exchange is determined by the values it threatens, the tuberculous poor walked past the mobile unit. The agency had nothing to offer them.

The health educators never really understood their failure. They blamed it upon the apathy and ignorance of the poor, an error they could never correct because they cut themselves off from the residents. The two women were afraid to enter the public housing units. They were warned about Negro gangs that snatched purses in broad daylight. One of them saw prostitutes beaten by collectors from the syndicate. To protect themselves, they stayed near the mobile unit and male technicians as much as possible. Since their few enduring contacts in the community were with social workers and tenant relations personnel, they did not acquire knowledge about the values and social structure of the slum which might have led to effective adaptations.

The health educators tried to reach the poor through a dozen local community improvement associations. Leaders were asked to use their influence with club members and neighbors in the campaign against tuberculosis. They did not provide the help they were asked to give. One health educator explained this failure by pointing to the values of the poor, as she understood them.

These little groups aren't effective in motivating residents. I planned with one of the social workers at the center to let a local group of Negroes handle the volunteer campaign in the northern section. The social worker had to do the job because nobody showed up. These people aren't concerned with TB or any other problem. They're happy with what they've got now.

Yet, the club the health educator had dismissed as ineffective had recently persuaded city officials to board up deteriorated buildings in the neighborhood, conducted a highly successful garden contest, and organized a voter registration drive in anticipation of the fall election. Other groups in the area were involved in similar undertakings, obtaining crossing guards for a busy intersection near the school, closing a tavern that sold to teenagers, and providing recreation programs for children. Community leaders were certainly not content: most were actively attacking the important problems of the community. But the health educators offered too little to divert their attention from what they considered urgent. Ironically, the health educators did not recognize the leaders' efforts to alleviate overcrowding or improve sanitation as important contributions to tuberculosis control. So they lost an opportunity to incorporate the X-ray program into valued, ongoing efforts.

Initially, the health educators thought they could reach the 17,000 public housing residents through the municipal housing authority and the building committees organized by tenant relations personnel. They soon found, however, that in most buildings the committees no longer existed or were small and hopelessly ineffective. One health educator interpreted the failure of the building committees in this way:

> The building committees didn't do much for us. Only five or six people in an entire building show up for a meeting. The residents don't even know enough to show up for these meetings which concern the living conditions and problems they have. They're just ignorant.

Members of the building committees explained their failure to encourage the residents to participate in the tuberculosis control program in another way. They felt "used" by the municipal housing authority and resentful toward organizations that tried to approach the residents through the building committee, no matter how worthy the cause. Hostility toward the housing authority and its functionaries is evident in this comment of a former building committee president:

> They (tenant relations personnel) give us ten dollars at Christmas, pat us on the back, and expect us to keep the residents in line. If they would spend more time taking care of the building and less time trying to organize us and control us, they'd have less trouble.

To have worked effectively in the public housing units would have pitted the tuberculosis agency against the municipal housing authority, a price it was unwilling to pay.

As employees of a voluntary health agency, the health educators' freedom to enter exchange relations with the poor was not only limited by their failure to understand the values of the impoverished but also by the constraints the agency placed upon them. Health educators were expected to contact social workers and tenant relations personnel, distribute the pamphlets and posters provided, and recruit and supervise volunteers for the mobile unit. Health educators were *not* to become involved with controversial leaders or organizations. The agency was dependent upon a complex network of relationships with city clinics, hospitals, sanatoriums, boards of health and the like. Alignment with indigenous leaders, who criticized or fought these important working partners, threatened the agency's security. Furthermore, the agency's operating expenses were met by voluntary contributions from the public, and adverse publicity growing out of controversy impaired its image.

As a consequence of the foregoing, the health educators could not avoid working through the ineffective building committeees because the tuberculosis agency had already asked housing authority officials for cooperation. They could not cooperate with indigenous leaders in exchange for support of the tuberculosis campaign for fear of becoming enmeshed in controversy. They could not confer prestige upon community leaders by asking them to serve on the steering committee, since these positions were filled by prominent city officials and civic leaders. Unlike the political bosses, they had no jobs to offer.

A HEALTH EDUCATOR ON SKID ROW: A SUCCESS

The agency's X-ray program on Skid Row was directed at some 9,000 men in two blighted areas near the Loop. In both districts are found the familair establishments catering to the needs of the "down-and-out," men's hotels, bars, seedy restaurants, hiring halls (called "slave markets"), and missions. On West Madison Street, the pensioners, the maimed and the derelicts are joined by a few Negro families near the district's western limit. On Clark Street, addicts, homosexuals, prostitutes, and criminals are more common. On both streets, ties to family, property, and local organizations that structure social life in the slums are almost nonexistent. In their place are the clusters of men found around the bars or hotel entrances: social organization on Skid Row is found on the street.

The men on Skid Row are confronted with about every problem social workers have ever faced. Divorce, desertion, rejection, and failure are common experiences of the past. Alcoholism, drug addiction, and mental and physical illness are common in the present. The death rate on Chicago's Skid Row is higher than rates in India or Africa. Tuberculosis is the primary or contributing cause in many instances, as one of every thirty men on the street is believed to have an active case of the disease.

The agency responded to the seriouness of the TB problem on Skid Row by sending a mobile X-ray unit, two technicians, a health educator and volunteers to the area for eight hours every day during an entire six week period. No other part of the city received as much attention. By the end of the summer, 7,210 X-rays had been taken, uncovering 268 suspects. This was an unqualified success by any standard voluntary tuberculosis agencies use.

The agency's program on Skid Row was unlike that used in other parts of the city. The health educator, who had worked on Skid Row for the past fourteen years, was prepared for his job by his past experiences as boxer, policeman, and entertainer, rather than by academic training. He enjoyed more freedom from agency direction than any other health educator in the organization; the agency had no other health educator who was qualified or willing to work in this district. Furthermore, constraints that bound the agency and its health educators in other parts of the city were, in part, suspended here. Extreme measures were called for on Skid Row and, if the health educator erred, the agency could hardly be blamed. Thus, the health educator was not required to give speeches on tuberculosis, use posters or handbills, or operate through the missions. The resulting program reflected his understanding of the culture of poverty.

The health educator did not expect most Skid Row habitués to be interested in tuberculosis. The men were primarily concerned with getting a quarter for a drink, finding a place to sleep, turning up something to eat or even with psychological problems like winning acceptance or living with fear or guilt. He expected resistance from men who were suspicious of outsiders and dreaded confinement in a sanatorium. He accepted as natural the point of view of a man who refused an X-ray with these words:

If I took an X-ray and you found out I had TB, it'd be your public duty to send me to a place and get me cured, wouldn't it? No sir! I've seen everything, I've done everything, and I've had everything. Why should I want you to fix me up to live a little longer?

Since the health educator accepted these values as given, he was able to develop exchange relationships with the men.

While the other health educators spent most of their time at the mobile X-ray unit or with social workers and tenant relations personnel, the Skid Row health educator was on the street, in the bars and hotels, and at the missions. He was visible, and he was known. He spoke their language, the *language of physical contact*. When he talked to the men, his hand was always on someone's shoulder or at their elbow. A joke ended with a clap on the back or a punch on the arm. When a fight broke out near the X-ray unit, he stepped between the men and pushed them apart, and if he could stop the fight in no other way, he entered in. This was the language of the street understood by those who belonged.

The health educator did not talk about health, tuberculosis or even taking X-rays. The men on the street knew what the health educator wanted and complied with his wishes. He repaid their favor by joining their company, for he was an entertaining companion. He loaned them money, gave them a pair of trousers or a shirt or bought them a drink. (With respect to the latter, he explained, "They're not going to quit drinking because I don't buy them a glass of wine.") Some of the men worked as volunteers at the unit and were repaid with a free lunch and a pack of cigarettes. Others served as barkers for the X-ray unit or protected the women volunteers in exchange for a ride around town in the health educator's flashy automobile. While other health educators sought to involve volunteers from the PTA or Eastern Star, the educator on Skid Row typically invited the girls living in a home for unwed mothers, who enjoyed getting out of the house for the day.

He used the mobile unit like a traveling sideshow, making the rounds of bars and hotels. The unit became the center of activity on the street whenever it was present in contrast to those unobtrusively parked in other parts of the city. Some days men who were X-rayed were given a hamburger or donuts and milk as they came out of the truck. Large crowds gathered on the sidewalk or men leaned out of windows to listen to a combo from the musician's union that played at the unit in the afternoons.

These simple, effective devices were possible because the health educator understood the values of the men on Skid Row and its social organization, and used his contacts with a mission, a milk company and the local musicians' union to meet their needs. They returned his favors by taking an X-ray.

This effective approach to the poor on Skid Row could easily fail if applied in other parts of the city, just as the inadequate program used in the slums behind the Gold Coast might succeed in the suburbs. The specifics of the program, as such, are less important than the establishment of meaningful exchange relations between the tuberculosis control agency and its clientele. . . . Before a meaningful exchange relation can be established on a street or in a jail, health educators must have an intimate familiarity with the values of the poor and the social structure of the slum as well as an awareness of their own values. Agency directors, in turn, should reappraise the organizational constraints imposed upon their field workers.

EPILOGUE ON
THE WAR ON
POVERTY

Several *important bills geared toward the reduction of poverty became law in the late summer and fall of 1965. The Senate authorized $1.65 billion for the Office of Economic Opportunity to extend the war against poverty through the next fiscal year. President Johnson signed a bill permitting rent subsidies from public funds for low-income families. With the passage of the Medicare Bill providing hospitalization and limited medical services for aged an important piece of legislation has been added to the Social Security Act.*

Among the practical achievements of the war on poverty project "Head Start" deserves first place. During the summer months about 2,500 communities created 13,400 centers to help poor children overcome some of the disadvantages of their background so that they would be better able to adjust to school. Starting this fall the project will be placed on a full year's basis. President Johnson emphasized repeatedly that the success of the project warrants this, although it is much too early for a general evaluation. Naturally, the project has been under criticism. In an article in The Reporter *of May 5, 1965, Barbara Carter quotes an interview with Martin Deutsch who has been developing experimental nursery school techniques for the past six years especially geared towards helping underprivileged children. The Head Start project is very much indebted to Dr. Deutsch. The difficulty has been mainly in translating a carefully designed experimental project into a crash project with insufficient funds, poorly trained people—often just a week's course in connection with a higher institution of learning—inappropriate or too few toys and teaching tools, and no provisions for follow up. There is danger that if the demonstration project does not prove that the children in it are learning better in school, the sceptics may discard it as useless, whereas it could become a major step forward in preschool education. The decision to continue the project for another year may be helpful, providing the staff can be found (many of the personnel during the summer were teachers) and provisions for careful evaluation are made. If nothing else the medical check-up and attention the children receive and the healthy breakfast they are fed are of great merit.*

As to other operations there are at present about 40 job centers in urban and rural areas with about 13,000 youngsters between 16 and 22 years of age placed there for training in job and social skills. Riots in some of the federal centers (which were to be expected) made headlines and may easily distort the potential merits of the centers in the mind of the general public.

The Vista program, volunteers contributing their services for a year for a modest subsistence allowance, has had a slow start. A local agency or a group must petition OEO for Vista volunteers, and the governor of the state must give his permission. About 300 volunteers have been working this summer in slum areas, on Indian reservations, in the Head Start program and in similar work assignments. The target for next year is 4,000 volunteers.

As was to be expected the "War on Poverty" has come under much criticism and has in part become a political football. A general criticism pertains to the danger of misleading the public as to the intent of the program. Herbert Hill, Labor Secretary of the NAACP, pointed out in a letter to The New York Times of July 29, 1965, that the allotment of somewhat over ¾ billion for the current fiscal year does not even equal the annual expenditures for public and private welfare expenses in New York City. Furthermore, the social consequences of how the money is spent are of greatest importance.

He writes, "Programs that train people for jobs that do not exist, or for occupations that help perpetuate the traditional concentration of minority racial groups in unskilled jobs . . . serve to intensify the growing alienation of those who come to believe they have been victims of a hoax. . . . Anti poverty programs have too frequently become extensions of old welfare programs that only subsidize the marginal life of the ghetto. . . . Allocation of vastly increased funds together with the development of new dynamic social concepts . . . will make a real war against poverty possible."

The largest conflict over the anti-poverty program centers around political and power issues. Two issues especially have aroused the widest interest and controversy. They are the questions of who should pass out the anti-poverty funds, and reap the political and power rewards, and who should sit on the policy making local Boards. The Senate during this summer has intensively debated the governors' power to veto the community programs for their states; it is feared that Republican governors might veto programs in mainly Democratic communities and so prevent the Democrats from reaping the political fruits of successful projects. The Senate therefore abolished the governors' vetoes for all projects except job corps and requests for Vista visitors.

In the cities themselves danger exists that poverty projects will be used to extend the power of City Hall and to create highly paid jobs for faithful political followers. The composition of the antipoverty local community action Boards that set policies and control finances has been under hot debate. Federal law requires that the Boards should have the widest representation; there must be representatives of governmental agencies, of private welfare and health organizations, of churches, etc., and "maximum feasible involvement of the poor themselves." What constitutes maximum involvement is open to the widest interpretation. One form of involvement is the hiring and training of poor people by local anti-poverty organizations to fulfil a variety of functions and jobs, from manual laborers to case aids in welfare agencies and interpreters of the programs. An additional, more complicated and controversial type of participation concerns the representation of poor neighborhoods through indigenous persons. Valid questions arise as to selection. Should it be done from neighborhood groups in the slums? *The poor with few execep-tions lack formal organization.* How can people who have been left out of any decision-making process be stirred into meaningful political activity? If this can be done will it mean a shift away from political power and bossism? The latter is exactly what is feared and it has in many large cities delayed effective planning and action. Most mayors want to keep control firmly in City Hall. They give as reason that elected officials are already representing the poor along with other citizens. Furthermore, since federal financing at the 90 per-cent level is scheduled to drop to 50 percent in 1967, local government will have to add the rest and should therefore have the power. There are a few cities where poor neighbor-hoods have an adequate representation (Sacramento, Cali-fornia gave a majority vote to the representatives of its target areas), in others, the Board and its policies are dominated by the Mayor. Saul Alinski, the successful organizer of the Chicago Woodlawn district, has shown that the poor can be organized and are capable of leadership and self-determina-tion. He believes (as quoted in *The New York Times of July,* 21) "that the big issue is not how many of the poor are sitting on the anti-poverty Boards or Councils, but who picks them, since representation requires an organized base. The struggle is basically between the power structure and militant inde-pendent groups." Whether and how these conflicts will be resolved and whether meaningful involvement of the poor is possible without militant action is one of the chief challenges of the war on poverty.

SELECTED BIBLIOGRAPHY

Bagdikian, Ben H., *In the Midst of Plenty.* Beacon Press, 1964, and Signet Book. A journalistic report of many aspects of poverty.

Bremner Robert F., *From the Depths.* New York University Press, 1956. A thorough study of our changing attitudes towards pov-erty from the early 1800s to the great depression.

Caplovitz, David, *The Poor Pay More.* Free Press, 1963. Documen-tary evidence of the relatively high costs of living in the slums.

Conference on Economic Progress, *Poverty and Deprivation in the United States*. Washington, 1962. The plight of two-fifths of a nation described in charts and statistics. Reform proposals.

Harrington, Michael, *The Other America*. Macmillan, 1963. Powerful description of the lives of the poor. Instrumental in bringing about the "War on Poverty."

Journal of Marriage and Family Living. Entire issue of November, 1964. Contains many valuable articles.

Hunter, Robert, *Poverty*. Macmillan, 1904. Harper & Row, Torchbooks, 1965. A classic on poverty in America, newly published with comments of Peter d'A. Jones.

Kolko, Gabriel, *Wealth and Power in America*. F. A. Praeger, New York, 1962. An analysis of income distribution.

May, Edgar, *The Wasted Americans*. Harper & Row, New York, 1964. A frank and critical account of the high costs of our welfare dilemma.

Miller, Herman P., *Rich Man, Poor Man*. Thomas Y. Crowell, New York, 1964. Discussion of latest trends in income distribution in the U.S.

"Our Enemy at Home." *The Nation*, June 1, 1965. A symposium of articles based on papers given at a seminar on poverty by the Institute of Government and Public Affairs, University of California.

Riessman, Frank, Jerome Cohen, and Arthur Pearl, *Mental Health of the Poor*, Free Press of Glencoe, 1964. A collection of 58 essays and research reports, many of them showing the inadequacy of present methods of treatment of the poor.

Schorr, Alvin L., *Slum and Social Insecurity*. (U.S. Government Printing Office, 1963.) A critical summary of research and current programs in the field of relocation and slum clearing.

Shostack, Arthur B., and William Gomberg, eds. *New Perspectives on Poverty*. Prentice-Hall, 1965. A collection of 19 articles on contemporary issues.

INDEX